Video Compression Techniques

Wolfgang Effelsberg is Professor of Computer Science at the University of Mannheim. He studied Electrical Engineering at Darmstadt University of Technology and holds a PhD in Computer Science. Before joining the University of Mannheim he held research positions in the U.S. and at IBM's European Networking Center in Heidelberg. The focus of his research work is on multimedia communications and multimedia content analysis.
He is on the editorial board of IEEE Multimedia and Kluwer Multimedia Tools and Applications, and a member of the program committees of ACM Multimedia and IEEE Multimedia. He has authored and co-authored numerous research papers on multimedia and networking topics.

Ralf Steinmetz is Professor of »Electrical Engineering and Information Technology« and »Computer Science« at the Darmstadt University of Technology. Since 1997 he is director of the GMD Integrated Publication and Information Systems Institute (IPSI) in Darmstadt.
He studied and holds a PhD in electrical engineering. He worked for IBM Heidelberg for several years, where he established and managed a Europen Media Center.
He has served as editor and member of several editorial boards of international journals. As general chair of ACM, IEEE, GI and ITG conferences and as author/coauthor of many papers he contributed to the multimedia and networking research community.

Wolfgang Effelsberg · Ralf Steinmetz

Video Compression Techniques

 dpunkt.verlag

Wolfgang Effelsberg
E-mail: effelsberg@pi4.informatik.uni-mannheim.de

Ralf Steinmetz
E-mail: Ralf.Steinmetz@KOM.tu-darmstadt.de

Editor: Dr. Michael Barabas
Copy Editing: Andy Ross, Heidelberg
Cover Design: Helmut Kraus, Düsseldorf
Printing: Koninklijke Wöhrmann B.V., Zutphen, Niederlande

Die Deutsche Bibliothek – CIP-Einheitsaufnahme

Video compression techniques. / Wolfgang Effelsberg ; Ralf Steinmetz. – Heidelberg :
dpunkt-Verl.
   ISBN 3-920993-13-6
   Buch. – 1. Aufl. – 1998 gebunden
   CD-ROM. – 1. Aufl. – 1998

Copyright © 1998 dpunkt – Verlag für digitale Technologie, Hüthig GmbH
Ringstrasse 19
69115 Heidelberg
Germany

Preface

Integrated multimedia systems process text, graphics, and other discrete media as well as digital audio and video streams. In an uncompressed state, non-trivial amounts of graphics, and audio and video data, especially moving pictures, require storage and digital network capacities not likely to be available in the near future. Hence, video compression has become a key component of any multimedia system or application. A plethora of techniques and related implementations already exist, while the development of more refined techniques and implementations is continuing.

This book aims to assist practitioners, developers, and researcher with a comparative overview on the fundamentals as well as the performance of the most widely deployed video compression techniques. Much of today's literature is either superficial or dedicated to one of the above-mentioned compression techniques, or loaded with mathematical details. In this book, we try to present an introduction and overview of current technologies, with an eye towards understanding their advantages and disadvantages, and their suitability for today's and tomorrow's multimedia systems.

A brief motivation behind the need for compression is followed by the essential requirements for these techniques as related to multimedia systems and applications. As most of these techniques apply the same principles, namely the fundamentals of source, entropy, and hybrid coding, these are explained in detail. Based on a general framework of the steps encountered in a compression system – data preparation, processing, quantization, and entropy coding – this book outlines details of the techniques developed by ITU-T (such as H.261, also called px64) and H.263, by ISO such as JPEG, MPEG, the color cell compression approach, and compression based on wavelets and fractals. A detailed section is devoted to understanding the crucial quality/bit rate trade-off, with many concrete examples. A companion CD-ROM visualizes the effects of different algorithms and their parameters on image quality and bit rate.

The initial version of this book (without any comparisons of compression schemes) is based on the authors work published as [74]. Thanks to the publisher we were allowed to refine the compression topic making use of our already available material.

Long days and nights were spent on the production of our experimental results. We would like to thank Tino von Roden at the University of Mannheim who did all of this work; without his dedication and deep understanding of the algorithms and implementation code this book would not have been possible. Also, we would like to thank Ralf Keller and Torsten Milde for allowing us to use text and images from their books. Part of this work at the Darmstadt University of Technology is supported by a grant of the Volkswagen-Stiftung, Hannover, Germany.

Mannheim/Darmstadt, July 1998 *Wolfgang Effelsberg, Ralf Steinmetz*

Table of Contents

List of Figures

List of Tables

1 Introduction

A multimedia system is characterized by the computer-controlled integrated generation, manipulation, presentation, storage, and communication of independent digital information [45], [46]. This information is most often coded in *continuous* – time-dependent – media (e.g., audio, video) as well as in *discrete* – time-independent – media (e.g., text, graphics). The storage of uncompressed graphics, audio and video data requires considerable capacity which in the case of uncompressed video is often not available, even with today's CD-ROM or DVD technology. The same is true for multimedia communications: A very high bandwidth, reserved exclusively for a single point-to-point communication, is necessary for the transfer of uncompressed video data over digital networks. Such a link is expensive and in many cases not available at all. In the interest of connectivity and efficiency, most multimedia systems handle digital video and audio data streams in *compressed form.*

In the early nineties a variety of compression techniques were developed that are in part competitive and in part complementary [3], [4], [6], [17], [18], [30]. While many of them are already in use in today's products, promising new methods are under development. Fractal image compression [5] and wavelets are gaining importance, but the most important compression techniques today are JPEG (for still images [36], [50], H.261 for video [27], [41], and MPEG for video and audio [24], [34]. Proprietary developments include DVI (for still images, audio, and video [12]), Intel's Indeo, Microsoft's Video for Windows, IBM's Ultimotion Matinee, Apple's QuickTime, and DigiCipher II developed by General Instruments Corp. and AT&T. MPEG-IV introduces the notion of object-oriented coding and compression, i.e., a technique where more of the semantics of the original image are preserved, and different pieces of the image can be encoded with different algorithms and different resolution. In the opinion of the authors, the future is still open, providing new techniques for all kinds of applications. This book focuses on well-established and innovative compression techniques, with an emphasis on standardized (non-proprietary) schemes.

For related projects, additional details and applications of compression schemes in e.g., communications, media processing and security please have a look ar our web pages:

http://www.informatik.uni-mannheim.de/informatik/pi4/
http://www.kom.e-technik.tu-darmstadt.de/
http://www.darmstadt.gmd.de/ipsi/

1.1 High Volumes of Data: the Motivation for Compression

Images require considerably more storage space than text, and audio and video are even more demanding in terms of data storage and bit rate. With some specific numbers, we want to illustrate the transition from simple text to full-motion video, and motivate the need for compression. To ensure comparability of the different media, the following calculations are based on a typical image format of 640×480 pixels on a screen.

❑ For the representation of text, most computers in the Western hemisphere use one byte per character. If a page has 55 lines of 80 characters its representation requires 35 200 bits.

❑ For the presentation of vector graphics, a typical still image is composed of 500 lines [6]. Each line is defined by its horizontal position, its vertical position, and an 8-bit attribute field. The horizontal axis is represented using 10 bits ($\log_2(640)$) and the vertical axis is coded using 9 bits ($\log_2(480)$).

❑ In very widely used color display modes, each pixel of an image can be represented in one of 256 different colors contained in the current color map, therefore we need one byte per pixel.

The next examples address continuous media and derive the amount of storage or bit rate required for one second of playback.

❑ An uncompressed audio signal in telephone quality is sampled at 8 kHz and quantized at 8 bits per sample. This leads to a data stream of 64 kbit/s.

❑ An uncompressed stereo audio signal in CD quality is sampled at a rate of 44.1 kHz and is quantized at 16 bits per sample. For two channels we need 1.411 Mbit/s.

❑ The European PAL standard defines a television signal of 625 lines with an aspect ratio of 4:3 of frame rate and a 25 frames per second. The luminance and the color difference signals are encoded separately. The resulting digital data streams are transformed using 4:2:2 sampling. In the CCIR 601 studio standard for digital video a sampling rate of 13.5 MHz is used for the luminance Y. The sampling rate for the chrominance components (R-Y and B-Y) is less, 6.75 MHz, because precision in chrominance is visually not as important to the human eye as precision in luminance. The result is a uniform 8-bit coding of each sample, i.e., (13.5 MHz + 6.75 MHz + 6.75 MHz) × 8 bit = 216 Mbit/s.

❑ HDTV doubles the number of lines and uses an aspect ratio of 16:9. As a result the data rate increases by a factor of 5.33 compared to today's TV, to 1 151 Gbit/s.

❑ A sequence of digital computer images (e.g., digitally produced video) might have a size of 640×480 pixels and run at 25 frames per second. For true colors we encode the R, G, and B components with 8 bits each (this is the empirically derived limit of the resolution of the human eye). This leads to a bit rate of 7 373 Mbit/s.

The storage and throughput requirements of a computer system that processes still images and in particular continuous media are illustrated by these few examples. We conclude that the processing of uncompressed video streams in a multimedia system requires secondary storage at least in the gigabyte range, and in the megabyte range for buffers in main memory. It also requires networks providing megabit data rates for each application. Although this is technically feasible with modern hardware, it is not economically reasonable. As we will see, the use of appropriate compression techniques considerably reduces the data transfer rates without much loss in quality [35], [42], and research, development, and standardization have progressed very quickly in the last few years [4].

1.2   Application-Specific Requirements

Compression in multimedia systems is subject to certain constraints. The *quality* of the coded, and later on, decoded data should be as good as possible. The *compression rate* should be as high as possible. In order to facilitate a cost-effective implementation, the *complexity* of the technique used should be minimal. And the *delay* introduced on a data link should be as short as possible. All modern compression methods are compromises between these goals.

Each multimedia application poses specific requirements. One can distinguish between requirements for applications in a *dialogue* mode and those in a *retrieval* mode. Some techniques are better suited for dialogue applications, with the same (symmetric) effort for compression and decompression and a short delay; an example is H.261, optimized for video conferencing. Other techniques are optimized for use in retrieval applications, i.e., for video servers where more time and effort may be spent during off-line compression in favor of fast online retrieval and decompression; an example is MPEG.

A *dialogue* application mandates consideration of the following requirements based on characteristics of human perception:

❑ The end-to-end delay should not exceed 150 ms (for compression and decompression). A delay in the range of 50 ms should be achieved in order to support 'face-to-face' dialogue applications. These 50 ms relate to the delay introduced by compression and decompression only. The overall end-to-end delay additionally comprises the latency in the network, in the processing within the end systems, and in the data transfer to and from the respective input and output devices.

A typical *retrieval* application has the following requirements:

❏ Fast forward and reverse with simultaneous display should be possible.

❏ Random access to a single image and/or audio frame of the data stream should be possible. This access should be faster than in a conventional CD digital audio system so as to maintain the interactive character of the application. Random access in 0.5 s would be a good value.

❏ For audio and video editing decompression should be possible without the knowledge of other data units. This allows the stream to be cut anywhere without re-computing neighboring frames.

The following requirements apply to both *dialogue* and *retrieval* mode:

❏ In order to support scalable video in different systems, it is necessary to define a format independent of frame size and video frame rate.

❏ Several different audio and video data rates should be supported. Thus, depending on specific system conditions, the data rates can be adjusted.

❏ It must be possible to synchronize audio with video data, as well as with other media.

❏ It should be possible to generate data on one multimedia system and reproduce them on another system. The compression technique should be compatible. Compatibility is relevant in the case of tutoring programs available on CD, for example; it allows different users to read the data on different systems, making them independent of the manufacturer. As many applications exchange multimedia data over communication networks, the compatibility of compression algorithms is a must. This is why standardization bodies such as ITU-T and ISO have established committees for audio, image, and video compression. The work of these committees has been quite successful, and the standards are now very widely accepted.

Many detailed examples for bit rates, delays, and other requirements for typical multimedia applications can be found in [26], [10], [22].

1.3   Examples on CD-ROM

Many fundamental ideas in modern compression technology can be demonstrated with examples. For this reason, this book comes with a CD-ROM, containing a collection of still images and short video clips. For each example the original image or video clip is included as well as various compressed versions, showing typical artifacts, etc. To benefit fully from this book, the reader should have access to a PC or workstation equipped with a CD-ROM drive, a WWW browser understanding HTML and the compression formats under consideration, and a color display with a resolution of at least 1024x768 pixels.

2 Fundamentals of Data Compression

To best comprehend the wide variety of compression techniques, it is a good idea to differentiate clearly between the various approaches by categorizing them, and to provide a reference architecture describing the principal processing steps. In this chapter, we will address these issues.

2.1 Entropy Coding, Source Coding, and Hybrid Coding

Coding techniques can be classified into the categories shown in Table 2-1. For their use in multimedia systems we distinguish between entropy coding, source coding, and hybrid coding. Entropy coding is a *lossless* process; it can be used for any type of data stream, and the decompressed stream is identical to the original. In contrast, source coding takes advantage of the properties of the human eye and ear, and is a *lossy* process. Most multimedia systems combine the two into hybrid coding techniques.

Entropy Coding	run-length coding
	vector quantization
	pattern substitution
	Huffman coding
	arithmetic coding
Source Coding	interpolation and subsampling
	transformation
	differencing
	DWT (wavelets)
	IFS (fractals)
Hybrid Coding	JPEG
	H.261, H.263
	MPEG

Table 2-1: A classification of coding techniques for multimedia systems

Entropy coding is a technique that disregards the specific characteristics of the stream. The data to be compressed is considered to be a sequence of bits, and the semantics of the data is ignored. An example is run-length coding. It is used to compress data in file systems, or still images in the Telefax standards. It is also used as a step in hybrid video or audio coding algorithms.

Source coding takes the semantics of the data into account. The degree of compression it affords depends on the data content. In lossy compression techniques, a one-way relation exists between the original data stream and the decoded data stream; the data streams are similar but not identical. Good source coding techniques make extensive use of the specific characteristics of the stream. For example, in the case of speech, a transformation from the time domain to the frequency domain followed by the encoding of the formants substantially reduces the amount of data (*formants* are defined as the maxima in the voice spectrum). In most cases, three to five formants suffice to reconstruct the original signal in the time domain. A major problem, however, is the correct reproduction of transitions between individual voice units in the time domain.

Another example of source coding with specific semantic knowledge is the use of spatial redundancies in still images. Other techniques transform the spatial domain into the two-dimensional frequency domain by means of the discrete cosine transform (DCT). Low frequencies define the 'average' color, high-frequency data correspond to sharp edges. Hence, low frequencies are much more important for photo-like images than higher frequencies, which is a key property used in DCT-based compression algorithms.

2.2   Fundamental Processing Steps

To help clarify the basic ideas behind hybrid coding schemes, we present a typical sequence of steps performed to compress a stream in Figure 2-1.

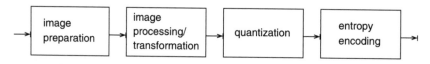

Figure 2-1: Fundamental processing steps in hybrid encoding

The following four steps describe compression based on the example of a still image.

1. *Image preparation* includes the analog-to-digital conversion and the generation of an appropriate digital representation of the data. A picture is typically divided into blocks of 8x8 pixels, each represented by a fixed number of bits.

2. *Image processing* is actually the first step in the compression process which makes use of sophisticated algorithms. For example, a transformation from the time to the frequency domain can be performed using a DCT. Another example is inter-frame coding, which uses a motion vector for each of the 8×8 blocks.

3. *Quantization* maps the exact numbers resulting from the previous step to *quantization intervals*, thereby reducing precision. The fewer quantization levels we have, the coarser is the output. In other words, the quantization factor trades off quality for bit rate. This is comparable to the effect defined by m-law and A-law encoding for audio [16].

4. *Entropy encoding* is usually the last step according to our reference scheme. It compresses a sequential digital data stream without loss, transforming it into a representation requiring fewer bits per data unit. For example, a long sequence of zeroes in a data stream can be compressed by specifying the number of occurrences followed by the digit 0.

Processing and quantization can be iterated several times in 'feedback' loops, as in the case of Adaptive Difference Pulse Code Modulation (ADPCM) for audio. Following compression, the digital data are packed into a data stream, often in the form of packets (or frames), each with a header. An identification of the compression technique used may be part of the header, and an error correction code may also be added. Figure 2-1 shows the compression algorithm applied to a still image; a similar procedure also can be applied to video or audio data.

Decompression is the inverse process. Specific encoders and decoders can function in various ways: *Symmetric* techniques, e.g., for dialogue applications, are characterized by approximately the same cost for encoding and decoding. In the case of *asymmetric* techniques, the decoding process is less costly than the encoding process. Asymmetric techniques are used for applications in which the compression process is performed only once, when plenty of time is available, whereas decompression is performed frequently and needs to be fast. For example, an audio-visual tutoring program will be produced once and will then be used by many students; therefore, it will be encoded once and decoded many times. In this case, efficient real-time decoding is a fundamental requirement whereas encoding need not be performed in real time. Asymmetric algorithms usually lead to much better compression rates than symmetric algorithms.

3 Basic Compression Techniques

We now present a number of well-known basic compression techniques used in computers for many different purposes. The hybrid compression techniques mentioned in the previous chapter all contain one or more of these basic algorithms.

3.1 Interpolation and Subsampling

The simplest compression techniques are based on interpolation and subsampling. Here, it is possible to make use of the specific physiological characteristics of the human eye or ear. For example, the human eye is more sensitive to differences in brightness than to differences in color. It is therefore reasonable to divide the image into YUV components (luminance Y and two chrominance difference signals U and V with $Y = 0.30R + 0.59G + 0.11B$, $U = B-Y$, $V = R-Y$) instead of using RGB components (red, green, blue). The components U and V can then be sampled at a lower resolution.

3.2 Run-Length Encoding

Sampled images and audio and video data streams often contain sequences of identical bytes; by replacing these sequences with the byte pattern to be repeated and providing the number of its occurrence, data can be reduced substantially. This is known as *run-length coding*, indicated by a special flag that does not constitute part of the data stream itself, similar to an ESCAPE character.

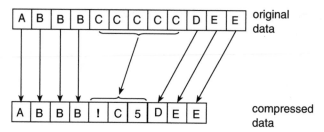

Figure 3-1: Example of run-length encoding

To illustrate run-length encoding, we define the exclamation mark "!" as such a special flag. A single occurrence of this exclamation mark is interpreted during decompression as the flag (two subsequent exclamation marks would be interpreted as an exclamation mark occurring within the data). The overall run-length encoding procedure can be described as follows. If the same byte occurs at least four times in a row, the number of occurrences is counted. The compressed data will contain the flag, the data byte and the number of occurrences. This allows the compression of sequences of 4 to 255 identical bytes into three bytes only; depending on the expected size of sequences more bytes could be used to encode the length. In Figure 3-1 the character "C" occurs five times and is "compressed" to three characters "!C5".

Run-length encoding is a generalization of zero suppression. Zero suppression assumes that just one symbol appears particularly often in the data. The blank in text or the zero in sequences of numbers are such symbols. All sequences of three or more blanks are replaced by a flag-byte and a byte that specifies the number of blanks of this sequence. Sequences of 3 to 255 bytes will be reduced to two bytes. Further variations are 'tabulators' used to substitute a specific number of zeroes (or blanks) depending on the relative position within a line, and the definition of different flag-bytes (tabulator bytes) to specify a different number of zero bytes (or blanks).

Obviously, for run-length encoding to be truly efficient, the data stream must contain long sequences of identical characters. When we design composite compression algorithms for images and video we can optimize the output of an earlier phase in our compression scheme to produce such long runs. The effect will be a subsequent run-length encoding phase that compresses well.

3.3   Vector Quantization

With vector quantization, a data stream is divided into blocks of n bytes each ($n > 1$). A predefined table contains a set of patterns. For each block, the table entry with the most similar pattern is identified. Each pattern in the table is associated with an index. Such a table can be multidimensional; in this case, the index will be a vector. This vector is used as the code for the block of bytes. The decoder uses the same table to generate an approximation of the original data stream. For further details and refinements, see [11].

3.4 Static Pattern Substitution and Diatomic Encoding

A technique that can be used for text compression substitutes single bytes for patterns that occur frequently. For instance, we can substitute the terminal symbols of high-level languages ('Begin', 'End', 'If'). Using an escape byte a larger number of patterns can be considered. This escape byte indicates that an encoded pattern will follow. The next byte is an index used as a reference to one out of 256 words. The same technique can be applied to still images as well as to video and audio; however, in these media, it is not always easy to identify small sets of frequently occurring patterns. Often it is better to perform an approximation that seeks the most similar rather than the same pattern.

Diatomic encoding is a variation based on a combination of two data bytes. This technique determines the pairs of bytes occurring most frequently. According to the analysis of the English language, the most frequent pairs are the following (note that the pairs 'E ', 'T ', 'A ', and 'S ' contain blanks):

'E ', 'T ', 'TH', 'A ', 'S ', 'RE', 'IN', and 'HE'

The replacement of these pairs by special single bytes that do not occur in the text reduces data by more than 10%.

3.5 Dynamic Pattern Substitution, Lempel–Ziv Encoding

The situation is different if we have no prior knowledge of the sequences of symbols occurring frequently. In this case, while encoding the stream, a code table must be constructed. As an example let us consider Figure 3-2. The sequences ABC and EE each occur twice; they are assigned the codes 1 and 2.

In general, it is difficult to extract the most appropriate sequences for dynamic pattern substitution, as this requires considerable processing. In our example, we could have chosen to code the sequence ABCEE as 1 and leave all other symbols unchanged. Figure 3-3 shows the result for that alternative. Note that the size of the encoded string is the same.

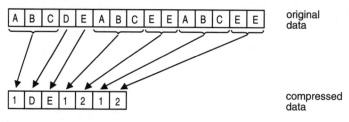

Figure 3-2: Dynamic pattern substitution, example 1

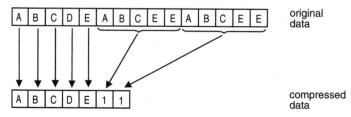

Figure 3-3: Dynamic pattern substitution, example 2

Lempel, Ziv, and Welch have developed an improved pattern substitution technique: the code table is constructed "on the fly". The basic idea is never to copy a sequence of bytes to the output stream that the encoder has seen before; instead each new sequence is stored as a new entry in the code table, and the index of that entry will be used to encode all future occurrences of the sequence.

The basic Lempel–Ziv algorithm works as follows: We scan the input stream, looking for the longest substring we have not seen so far. A code table (dictionary) is created on the fly; at any time t it contains all the substrings (prefixes) we have already seen. Let #i denote the ith index of the table, [w] the scan window containing the string w. Here is the pseudocode:

1. Initialize the code table with the elements of the alphabet, one entry for each character.
2. Initialize the scan window as empty: [ ].
3. Accept the next character K from the input stream and concatenate it with the scan window: [w]K
4. Do we have an entry for [w]K in the code table?
   - If yes, integrate K into the scan window: [w']:=[wK] and go to 3.
   - If no, add [w]K as a new entry to the code table, write the index of [w] to the output stream, set [w]:=[K] and go to 3.
5. When the end of the input stream is reached process [w] from left to right, choosing the longest possible substrings from the code table.

Let us now look at an example. Our alphabet is {A,B,C,D}. We compress the string ABACABA. In step 1 we initialize the code table:

#0 = A

#1 = B

#2 = C

#3 = D

In step 2 the scan window is set to [ ]. We now read A from the input stream and consider [ ]A = A. In step 4 we find A in the code table and set the scan window to [A]. Back to step 3 we read B and consider [A]B = AB. It is not contained in the code table, so we add AB as entry #4 to the code table, write #0 (for A) to the output stream and set the scan window to [B]. Back to step 3 we now consider BA, add it to the code table as #5, write #1 (for B) to the output stream, etc. The final code table will be

#0 = A

#1 = B

#2 = C

#3 = D

#4 = AB

#5 = BA

#6 = AC

#7 = CA

#8 = ABA.

The compressed stream will be #0 #1 #0 #2 #4 #0.

Remember that the code table is constructed dynamically, and is optimal for the input stream. There is no need to transmit the code table; the receiver/decoder can build it on the fly from the data stream and the initial code table (with one entry per single character of the alphabet). Note that compression gets better and better with larger code table entries; in practice the size of the code table is a parameter controlling the trade-off between speed and compression rate of the algorithm.

Lempel–Ziv encoding is used in the UNIX compress utility and in many other modern file compression programs.

3.6   Variable-Length Encoding

Characters (data bytes) do not have to be coded with a fixed number of bits. The Morse alphabet is based on this principle: frequently occurring characters are coded with shorter patterns. The code depends on the frequency of occurrence of single characters or sequences of data bytes. A variety of compression techniques are based on these statistical methods, the most prominent being Huffman encoding and arithmetic encoding.

With variable bit codes we have a new problem: it is no longer obvious where a code character ends. We cannot afford to reserve a specific bit pattern as a separator. Therefore we have to construct our code with the following property:

A code character must not be a prefix of another code character.

This property allows us to unambiguously parse the encoded stream.

3.6.1   Huffman Encoding

David Huffman has proposed an algorithm for constructing a variable-length code with this property [15]. In addition, his code is *optimal*: It creates the minimum number of bits for given probabilities of occurrence for each character.

To determine a Huffman code it is useful to construct a binary tree whose leaves represent the characters to be encoded. Each node of the tree is marked with the probability of occurrence of the characters belonging to its subtree.

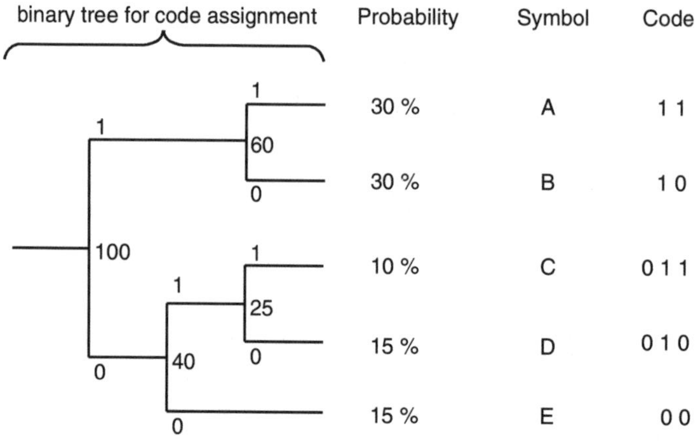

binary tree for code assignment	Probability	Symbol	Code
	30 %	A	1 1
	30 %	B	1 0
	10 %	C	0 1 1
	15 %	D	0 1 0
	15 %	E	0 0

Figure 3-4: An example for the creation of a Huffman code

The example in illustrates the process:

❑ The characters A, B, C, D, and E have the following relative probability of occurrence:

$$p(A) = 0.3; p(B) = 0.3; p(C) = 0.1; p(D) = 0.15; p(E) = 0.15$$

❑ The characters with the lowest probabilities, C and D are combined. The combined probability of their father node CD is 0.25. The edge from node CD to node C is assigned a 1, and the edge from CD to D is assigned a 0. This assignment is arbitrary; therefore, with the same data, different Huffman codes are possible.

❑ We now have to deal with the following nodes and probabilities:

$$p(A) = 0.3, p(B) = 0.3, p(CD) = 0.25, p(E) = 0.15$$

Again, the two nodes with the lowest probabilities are combined into a binary subtree, namely E and CD, and the combined probability of their father CDE is 0.40. The edge from CDE to CD is assigned a 1, and the edge from CDE to E a 0. If root nodes of different subtrees have the same probabilities, the trees with the minimal heights are combined. This keeps the code lengths more balanced.

❑ The following nodes and probabilities are now left:

$$p(A) = 0.3, p(B) = 0.3, p(CDE) = 0.4$$

The nodes with the smallest probabilities are A and B. They are combined into a binary tree; the combined probability of their root node AB is 0.6. The edge from AB to A is assigned a 1, and the edge from AB to B a 0.

❑ Two nodes are left:

$$p(AB) = 0.6, p(CDE) = 0.4$$

They are combined to a binary tree with the root ABCDE. The edge from ABCDE to AB is assigned a 1, the edge from ABCDE to CDE is assigned a 0.

Figure 3-4 also shows the resulting Huffman code:

$$code(A) = 11, code(B) = 10, code(C) = 011, code(D) = 010, code(E) = 00.$$

This scheme can be used to compress an arbitrary data stream without any loss. Note that no codeword is a prefix of another codeword so that the decoder can unambiguously parse the incoming bit stream. The simplest way to generate a bit stream for an image would be to code the pixels individually and read them line by line. Note that usually more sophisticated methods are applied, as described in the remainder of this book. The same Huffman table must be available for encoding and decoding, and it must be stored/transmitted in addition to the encoded data.

3.6.2   Arithmetic Encoding

In the 1980s researchers at IBM developed new coding algorithms based on an interesting observation: none of the coding schemes we have discussed so far can optimally adapt to given character probabilities because they encode each input character with an integer number of bits. Consider an alphabet {A, B, C} where p(A) = p(B) = p(C) = 1/3. It is obvious that the Huffman code is not optimal, in an information-theoretic sense, no matter how we assign 1- and 2-bit codewords to A, B, and C. As a solution they have proposed *arithmetic coding.*

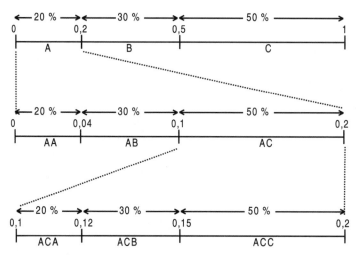

Figure 3-5: Example of arithmetic encoding

Figure 3-5 illustrates the basic idea of arithmetic encoding. Let us assume an alphabet {A, B, C}, with probabilities of occurrence p(A) = 0.2, p(B) = 0.3, and p(C) = 0.5. An initial interval with lower bound 0 and upper bound 1 is sub-divided according to these probabilities. In order to compute the code of a given input sequence (say, ACB), the interval of A is further divided according to the respective probabilities for the second character, C. The segment between lower bound 0 and upper bound 0.2 is further subdivided as shown on the second and third lines of Figure 3-5. ACB now has a lower bound of 0.12 and an upper bound of 0.15. In principle, the procedure is repeated recursively until the entire input string has been processed. This leads to an interval unambiguously representing the input string. Any number within that interval can now be used as the code for the string (usually the one with the smallest number of digits is chosen). In our example we might choose 0.13.

From an information theory point of view, arithmetic encoding is better than codes with integer numbers of bits per codeword; it can generate shorter codes for strings, and the total length of the encoded data stream is minimal. Unlike

Huffman coding, arithmetic coding does not encode each symbol separately but computes a code representing the entire string. Thus, an encoded data stream must always be read from the beginning, which rules out random access. In practice, arithmetic and Huffman coding often achieve similar average compression rates [47]. For a detailed discussion of arithmetic coding see [14].

3.7 Transform Encoding

Transform encoding pursues a very different approach: Data is transformed into another mathematical domain more suitable for compression. The inverse transformation must exist. The most familiar example is the Fourier transformation which transforms data from the time domain into the frequency domain. The most effective transformations for image compression are the *Discrete Cosine Transform* DCT (see Section 5.1.2) and also, to some extent, the *Fast Fourier Transform* FFT.

If we consider such transformations for image encoding, the original domain is a two-dimensional image, with each pixel represented by a gray-scale value or a color value (the latter often represented as a triple). Leaving out some of the pixels for compression is obviously not a good idea; it would be visually quite disturbing. In the transformed domain the image elements are represented by frequency coefficients: the "DC" coefficient describes the average gray value (resp. color), the higher-order coefficients correspond to sharper edges. If we sacrifice precision for the higher-order coefficients the visual effect is less detail at sharp edges in the image. For many applications this is visually much more acceptable than losing precision in the two-dimensional image domain.

3.8 Subband Encoding

Unlike general transformation encoding which transforms all data into another domain, selective frequency transformation subband coding considers a spectral selection of the signal in predefined frequency bands. The number of bands is an important criterion for quality. This technique is well suited for the compression of speech and often makes use of the FFT mentioned above for spectral filtering.

The principle of subband coding is illustrated in Figure 3-6. A filter bank subdivides the input frequencies, and a different quantizer/encoder is used for each subband. In our audio example we could use coarse quantization below 100 Hz and above 16 000 Hz, and finer quantization for the more audible subbands. The encoded data packets are multiplexed onto the output line. The decoder performs the inverse operations. For a detailed discussion of subband coding the reader is referred to [43]. An efficient subband coding scheme for video is described in [48].

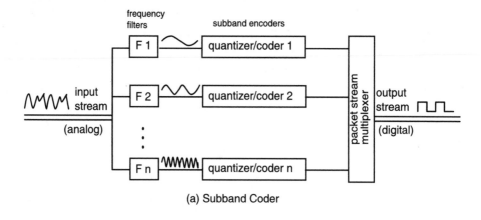

(a) Subband Coder

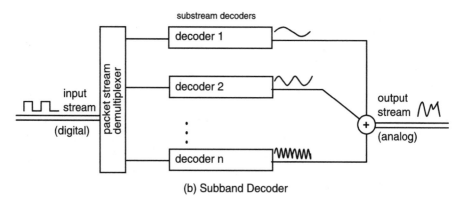

(b) Subband Decoder

Figure 3-6: The principle of subband coding

We can now ask under what circumstances subband coding is worthwhile. If the precision of the signal receiver is the same in all frequency ranges (or if the power distribution of the signal is even, and equally important), there is no gain with subband coding. This is shown in Figure 3-7 (a). If we can easily distinguish two levels of precision (resp. power) in two intervals, then two subbands are optimal (see Figure 3-7 (b)). A distribution like (c) would require many small subbands and thus considerable technical effort, but might be worthwhile, whereas for a distribution like (d) the gain would be minimal. We conclude that a very good understanding of the frequency spectrum under consideration is an important prerequisite for efficient subband coding.

Often the motivation behind subband coding is that the human eye or ear does not perceive signals equally well over the full frequency spectrum. For example, it is well known that the ear can hear frequencies from about 40 Hz to 20 000 Hz, but the lowest and highest parts of the spectrum require much higher energies to be audible, and precision is much worse. So we can encode the coefficients in those subbands with less accuracy, and thus fewer bits.

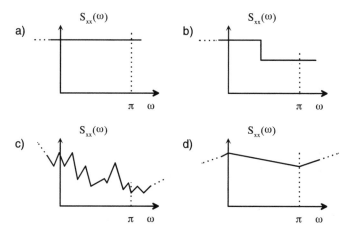

Figure 3-7: Various spectral power distributions (adapted from [43])

3.9 Differential Encoding

Instead of compressing single bytes or sequences of bytes separately, differential encoding can be used. This is also known as prediction or relative encoding. Consider the example of a sequence of characters whose values are clearly different from zero, but which do not differ much. In this case, encoding of the difference from the previous value would lead to compression.

The following explains this technique for different media:

❑ For still images, in the calculation of differences between nearby pixels or pixel groups, edges will lead to large values, whereas areas with similar luminance and chrominance are characterized by small values. With differential encoding a homogeneous area is characterized by a large number of zeroes that could be further compressed using run-length encoding.

❑ The use of relative coding in the time domain for video can lead to encoding of the differences from the previous frame. In newscast and video-telephone applications the background often remains the same for a long time, therefore, the 'difference' between subsequent images is very small, leading to a large number of zeroes in differential encoding.

❑ Audio techniques often apply Differential Pulse Code Modulation (DPCM) to a sequence of samples (see, e.g., [16]). It is not necessary to encode the absolute value of each sample with a large number of bits because audio signals change rather slowly. It is sufficient to represent only the first PCM-coded sample as a whole and all following samples as differences from the previous value.

❑ Delta Modulation (DM) is a modification of DPCM (see e.g., [16]). The difference between value i and value $i+1$ is encoded with one bit which indicates whether the signal increases or decreases. This results in an inaccurate coding of steep slopes.

Most of the compression techniques described so far are based on already known characteristics of the data, such as sequences of bytes occurring frequently or the probability of the occurrence of certain characters. An untypical sequence of characters will not be compressed well with these methods.

Adaptive compression techniques adapt a particular compression technique to the particular data to be compressed on the fly. This adaptation can be implemented in different ways. A prominent adaptive compression technique is adaptive DPCM (ADPCM). It is a 'follow-on' development of differential pulse code modulation (DPCM). Here, differences are encoded using a small number of bits (e.g., 4 bits). Therefore, either large transitions will be coded correctly (the four bits would represent the most significant bits of the differential value) or small changes are coded exactly (the DPCM encoded values are the least significant bits of the differential value). In the first case, the resolution of low audio signals would be insufficient, and in the second case, a loss of high frequencies would occur. ADPCM adapts automatically to the 'significance' for a particular data stream. Conceptually, ADPCM starts with a DPCM-encoded bit stream. The encoder divides the value of each DPCM sample by a suitable coefficient, and the decoder multiplies the compressed data by the same coefficient, i.e., the step size of the signal changes. The value of the coefficient is adapted to the DPCM-encoded signal by the coder. In the event of a signal with high frequency (i.e., steep slopes), very high DPCM coefficient values occur. The coder determines a high value for the coefficient. The result is a very rough quantization of the DPCM signal in passages with steep slopes. Low-frequency portions of such passages are encoded imprecisely. For a signal with low DPCM values, i.e., with few high frequencies, the coder will determine a small coefficient. Thereby, a good resolution of the dominant low-frequency signal portions is guaranteed. If high-frequency portions of the signal suddenly occur in such a passage a signal distortion in the form of a 'slope-overload' arises.

In most ADPCM schemes, the decoder calculates the coefficients dynamically from the ADPCM-encoded data stream. An audio signal with frequently changing frequency portions of extremely high or low frequencies turns out to be not very suitable for such an ADPCM encoding. In the G.700 series of standards, ITU-T has standardized a version of the ADPCM technique using 32 kbits/s for telephone applications; it is based on 4 bits per sample and an 8 kHz sampling rate.

3.10   Some Final Remarks

In addition to the basic compression techniques described in this chapter, some additional well-known techniques are being used today. Video compression techniques often use color lookup table (CLUTs) to achieve data reduction. For instance, in [23], [25], this technique is used in distributed multimedia systems. And a simple technique for audio is silence suppression: data is only encoded if the volume level exceeds a certain threshold. This can be seen as special case of run-length encoding.

ITU-T incorporated some of the basic audio coding schemes into the G.700 series of standards: G.721 defines the PCM coding for a quality of 3.4 kHz over 64 kbit/s channels. G.728 defines 3.4 kHz quality over 16 kbit/s channels. Reference [2] provides a more detailed description of various audio coding techniques. A detailed discussion of all these techniques would go beyond the scope of this introductory book.

In the following chapters, the most important work in the standardization bodies concerning image and video coding is outlined. We will discuss still image compression first and then turn to video compression.

4 Still Image Compression Techniques

In this chapter we discuss compression techniques for still images. We begin with older compression algorithms operating in the two-dimensional image space and proceed to current technology such as JPEG, compression based on fractals, and compression based on wavelet transforms.

4.1 Block Truncation Coding (BTC)

Before modern high-performance compression techniques for multimedia applications were designed, much simpler block-oriented compression schemes were very popular. In contrast to MPEG or JPEG, they do not use a Discrete Cosine Transform (DCT) but remain in the two-dimensional image space. The DCT is a complex and computationally very demanding mathematical function. As a consequence, software video players based on JPEG or MPEG tend to be slow, even on the most powerful CPUs available today, and it is generally assumed that these compression schemes only work well with hardware support. Simpler block-based bit manipulation schemes often yield a lower image quality but run much faster in software.

The classical Block Truncation Coding Algorithm is used in the compression of monochrome images. When compressing color images, it can be applied separately to the three color channels.

The first step of the algorithm is the decomposition of the image into blocks of size $n \times m$ pixels. Usually these blocks are quadratic with $n = m = 4$. For each block P, the mean value μ and the standard deviation σ are computed as follows:

$$\mu = \frac{1}{nm} \sum_{i=1}^{n} \sum_{j=1}^{m} P_{i,j}$$

$$\sigma = \sqrt{\frac{1}{nm} \sum_{i=1}^{n} \sum_{j=1}^{m} P^{2}_{i,j} - \mu^{2}}$$

where $P_{i,j}$ is the brightness of the pixel.

In addition, a bit array B of size $n \times m$ is calculated for each block. A one in this bit array indicates that the gray value of the corresponding pixel is greater than the mean value, a zero indicates that the value is smaller than the mean value:

$$B_{i,j} = \begin{cases} 1 \text{ if } P_{i,j} \geq \mu \\ \\ 0 \text{ else} \end{cases}$$

The decompression algorithm will know, based on the bit array, whether the pixel is darker or brighter than the average. Last, we need the two gray scale values for the darker and for the brighter pixels. These values a and b are calculated based on the mean value and the standard deviation, and are then stored together with the bit array:

$$a = \mu + \sigma\sqrt{p/q}$$
$$b = \mu - \sigma\sqrt{q/p}$$

Here, p and q are the number of pixels having a larger or smaller brightness, respectively, than the mean value of the block.

During the decompression phase, each block of pixels is calculated as follows:

$$P'_{i,j} = \begin{cases} a \text{ if } B_{i,j} = 1 \\ b \text{ else} \end{cases}$$

i.e., where the bit array shows a 1, the gray value a is used, and where it shows a 0, the value b is used.

Assuming that the original image used one byte per pixel, we had a storage requirement of 128 bits for each 4×4 block. The compressed block can be stored with 16 bits for the bit array plus one byte for each of the values a and b. Hence, we have a storage reduction from eight bits to two bits per pixel.

4.2 Color Cell Compression

If BTC is to be used for color images rather than for gray-scale images, the components (red, green, and blue, as well as chrominance and luminance) can be compressed separately. However, the Color Cell Compression (CCC) method promises a much better compression rate.

As for BTC, the image is divided into blocks called "color cells". The two values a and b are now indices into a color lookup table (CLUT).

The criterion for the bit array values is now the brightness of the corresponding pixel. The brightness of a pixel is computed in the following way, taking the human perception into account:

$$Y = 0.3P_{red} + 0.59P_{green} + 0.11P_{blue}$$

In other words, the intensities of the red, green, and blue components are weighted with their relative contribution to brightness, as perceived by the human eye. The mean value of each block can now be computed out of these brightness values (analogous to the BTC method). Let us define $P_{red,i,j}$ as the red component of $P_{i,j}$, $P_{green,i,j}$ as the green component, and $P_{blue,i,j}$ as the blue component. The next step is then to compute the color values of a_{red}, a_{green} and a_{blue}, as well as b_{red}, b_{green} and b_{blue}:

$$a_c = \frac{1}{q} \sum_{Yi,j \geq \mu} P_{c,i,j}, \quad b_c = \frac{1}{p} \sum_{Yi,j < \mu} P_{c,i,j} \text{ with } c = \text{red, green, blue}$$

Again, p and q are the number of pixels with a brightness larger or smaller, respectively, than the mean value. The bit array is computed as for BTC.

The color values $a = (a_{red}, a_{green}, a_{blue})$ and $b = (b_{red}, b_{green}, b_{blue})$ are now quantized onto a color lookup table. In this way, we get the values a' and b'. These values are stored together with the bit array (see Figure 4-1).

The decompression algorithm works analogous to the BTC method:

$$P'_{i,j} = \begin{cases} CLUT[a'] \text{ if } B_{i,j} = 1 \\ CLUT[b'] \text{ else} \end{cases}$$

where CLUT is the color lookup table.

If the CLUT has 256 entries the two values a' and b' can each be stored in one byte. Hence, the storage needed with CCC is two bits per pixel, as with BTC (to be more exact, we would have to add the storage needed by the CLUT, i.e., 256×3 bytes for the full image). The Color Cell Compression algorithm is illustrated in Figure 4-1.

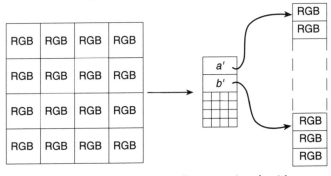

Figure 4-1: Illustration of the Color Cell Compression algorithm

Color Cell Compression is not only one of the best compression algorithms operating in the image domain, it is also one of the fastest. All calculations can be done without floating point operations, and the asymptotic complexity is

$$O\left(NM\left(1+\frac{\log k}{nm}\right)\right)$$

for an image size of $n \times m$ and of color lookup table size k. Decompression is also done without floating point operations with a complexity of $O(NM)$.

As in the case of the BTC algorithm, a number of possible improvements exist for CCC as well:

- ❑ If the two colors a and b are nearly equal, or one color dominates in frequency of occurrence, only one color is stored, and no bit array is needed.
- ❑ If an image contains large areas with only small differences in color, those areas may be encoded with larger blocks.
- ❑ For movies, cuboids may be used, with time as the third dimension, if the changes from frame to frame are small enough.

An extension of CCC based on the second idea is XCCC (Extended Color Cell Compression). For details, the interested reader is referred to [7].

4.3   Compression in the Telefax Standards

Another simple and straightforward approach to image compression is the use of run-length coding and Huffman coding for an image scanned in line by line. Such a technique will not be very efficient for photos with a fine resolution, but can be quite good for black-and-white or gray-scale input consisting mostly of text and line drawings and a lot of white space. In fact, the ITU-T standards for Telefax Group 3 and 4 are based entirely on such basic algorithms.

Let us take a closer look at the Group 3 compression standard. It was developed between 1980 and 1988, based on the following parameters:

- ❑ Two-tone (black-and-white) images of size A4
- ❑ Resolution 100 dots per inch
- ❑ 1728 samples per line
- ❑ transmission at 4800 bit/s over a telephone line.

We present a slightly simplified version of the Group 3 algorithm here. Figure 4-2 shows part of a line of black-and-white pixels. Obviously, runs will be much larger than 1 in most cases, and thus run-length encoding is efficient. Since we only consider black or white pixels, there is no need to encode a gray-scale or color value; the encoded line just consists of run lengths for alternating bits.

Run-length encoding: 4 3 1 1 2 1

Figure 4-2: Section from a scan line of a telefax document

From empirical analysis we know that the distribution of run lengths is not equal. Therefore the use of a variable-length code for the different sizes of runs is appropriate. The standard defines a modified Huffman code; Table 4-1 shows rows 0 to 20 of the code table. Note that run lengths occurring frequently are coded with very short codewords.

White run length	Codeword	Black run length	Codeword
0	00110101	0	0000110111
1	000111	1	010
2	0111	2	11
3	1000	3	10
4	1011	4	011
5	1100	5	0011
6	1110	6	0010
7	1111	7	00011
8	10011	8	000101
9	10100	9	000100
10	00111	10	0000100
11	01000	11	0000101
12	001000	12	0000111
13	000011	13	00000100
14	110100	14	00000111
15	110101	15	000011000
16	101010	16	0000010111
17	101011	17	0000011000
18	0100111	18	0000001000
19	0001100	19	00001100111
20	0001000	20	00001101000

Table 4-1: Modified Huffmann code in the Telefax standard (excerpt)

Since single bit errors would corrupt the entire image, the standard defines special control codes for re-synchronization, such as an EOL (end-of-line) codeword. For typical letters this simple compression scheme is quite efficient. For more details the reader is referred to [21].

4.4 JPEG

JPEG stands for Joint Photographic Experts Group, joint because the development of this standard was done jointly between ITU-T (the former CCITT) and ISO [50]. JPEG is a compression standard for continuous-tone still images. The compression algorithms can be used on both gray-scale and color images.

When the experts group discussed the advantages and disadvantages of lossless versus lossy compression, it became obvious that there were many important applications for both. For example, lossy compression is acceptable in most entertainment applications whereas it is often undesirable in medical imaging. In order to be applicable to a large number of applications, the JPEG standard comprises one lossless and three lossy modes:

❑ sequential
❑ hierarchical
❑ progressive
❑ lossless.

The mode most widely used is the sequential mode. The image is processed line by line, and the decoder has to decode the full image in any case. The sequential mode is illustrated in Figure 4-3.

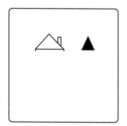  

Figure 4-3: JPEG decoding in sequential mode

JPEG is now used very widely throughout the industry. In particular, many images on the World Wide Web are encoded in JPEG, and JPEG decoders are available for all kinds of machines. However, in most decoders, only the *baseline method* is implemented. It is in fact a subset of the sequential mode. The baseline mode of JPEG is also the basis for intra-frame coding in H.261 and in MPEG, as we will see later.

4.4.1 Compression Principle

The JPEG *baseline* method works as follows. The image is subdivided into blocks of 8×8 pixels. Each block is encoded separately. The Discrete Cosine Transform (DCT) is applied. The resulting DCT coefficients are quantized, and finally the quantized DCT coefficients are encoded by an entropy encoder. Decompression proceeds in the inverse order. FDCT stands for *forward DCT*, IDCT stands for *inverse DCT*. The encoding and decoding process is illustrated in Figures 4-4 and 4-5.

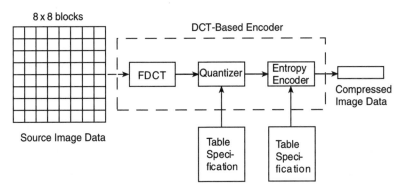

Figure 4-4: DCT-based JPEG encoder

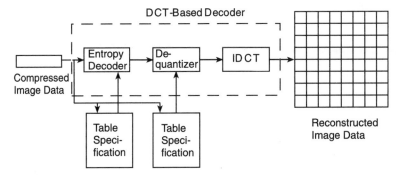

Figure 4-5: DCT-based JPEG decoder

4.4.2 The DCT Step

The Discrete Cosine Transform (DCT) falls into the category of transformation encodings, as discussed in Chapter 3. It is quite similar to a Fourier transform, mapping the data from a two-dimensional image domain to the frequency domain. The fact that it is *discrete* makes it especially suitable for an efficient computation.

The formula for the DCT step can be written as follows:

$$S_{vu} = \frac{1}{4}C_uC_v\sum_{x=0}^{7}\sum_{y=0}^{7} s_{xy} \cos\frac{(2x+1)u\pi}{16} \cos\frac{(2y+1)v\pi}{16}$$

with $C_u, C_v = \frac{1}{\sqrt{2}}$ for u, v = 0; $C_u, C_v = 1$ otherwise.

The result of the DCT step is a set of 64 DCT values (coefficients) for each block of the image.

4.4.3 Quantization

The quantization in JPEG is based on a quantization table with 64 entries, one for each DCT coefficient. A different quantization table can be specified for each application; it can be optimized for the characteristics of the display, the viewing distance, the amount of noise in the source, etc. Of course, the decoder must know the quantization table in use, and the table is thus transferred with the compressed data stream.

The equations for quantization and inverse quantization are:

$Fq(u,v) = Integer(Round(F(u,v)/Q(u,v)))$

$Fq^{-1}(u,v) = F(u,v)Q(U,v)$

where $F(u,v)$ is a DCT coefficient and $Q(u,v)$ is the quantization table entry.

4.4.4 Entropy Encoding

Entropy encoding is applied to achieve the shortest possible encoding for each (quantized) coefficient. For the baseline mode of JPEG, Huffman encoding is used. Typically, the input to the entropy encoder has a few non-zero and many zero coefficients. The non-zero coefficients tend to occur in the upper left-hand corner of the block, the zero coefficients in the lower right corner. In order to maximize the number of subsequent zeroes in the stream, a trick is used: the block of coefficients is not read out line-by-line, but in a zig-zag fashion (see Figure 4-6).

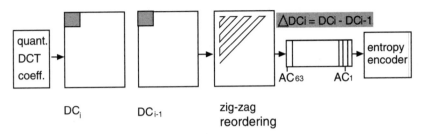

Figure 4-6: Encoding of DCT coefficients in JPEG

Each DCT coefficient is represented as a pair of symbols, symbol 1 containing a run-length and a size, and symbol 2 the amplitude. In symbol 1, the run-length encodes the number of *preceding* zero values, the size the number of bits used to encode the following amplitude. After representing each coefficient of the 8×8 block in this fashion, variable-length codes are assigned to each symbol: symbol 1 is encoded using a Huffman table, symbol 2 is simply a variable-length binary integer. This ensures close-to-optimum encoding without further loss of image quality.

4.4.5 Progressive Mode

In some applications, it is important to be able to serve users with different requirements for image resolution from the same image database. Rather than storing each image in different resolutions, compressed in sequential mode, the JPEG Progressive Mode can be used. Here, each new level of progression adds more detail to the image (also requiring a higher-resolution display and more decompression power on the receiver's side). The progressive mode of JPEG is illustrated in Figure 4-7. For the technical details of progressive encoding, the reader is referred to [37], or to the JPEG standard.

Figure 4-7: JPEG Progressive Mode

4.5   Image Compression with Fractals

Quite different from all the other coding schemes we have presented so far is image coding with *fractals*. It is based on the now-famous observation by Benoit Mandelbrot that many images are *self-similar*, i.e., more detail can be derived from repeating shapes occurring in an image at a finer granularity. For example, if we look at the coastline of the British isles from a satellite we see a rugged profile; if we look down at a part of the coast line from an airplane we perceive a similar profile at a much finer resolution. The mathematical functions describing such self-similar shapes are called *fractals*.

Fractals can be used for image compression if we take advantage of the self-similarity: a complex shape *A*, once coded for one area of the image, can be repeated easily by the decoder in other areas of the image. A similar shape *B* will typically occur in a different position and size, perhaps rotated and with a different contrast. We allow transformations that *skew, stretch, rotate, scale*, and *translate* a shape. In addition, *contrast* and *brightness* can be changed.

The fundamental idea of fractal coding is now to represent the derived version of a shape by a simple mathematical function (transform). The binary representation of the transform function will require many fewer bits than the repetition of the self-similar shape as a block of pixels elsewhere in the image.

The transformation process of mapping coarse-scale image features to finescale features is illustrated in Figure 4-8. In this example, the original block in the image on the left side is first averaged and subsampled and then rotated. Finally, the contrast is modified and the addition of an offset adjusts the transformed image block.

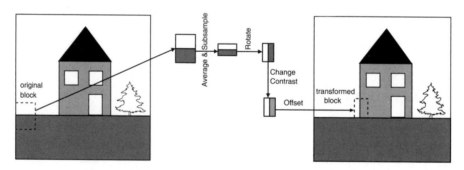

Figure 4-8: Mathematical transformation of an image block

An advantage of fractal coding is the possibility of computing the image at different levels of resolution, without using interpolation or the duplication of pixel values. The more iterations we execute when decompressing, the better the image quality will be. A major disadvantage of fractal coding is the fact that it is quite difficult to find self-similar regions in an image. This is a computationally intensive process, and thus fractal compression clearly falls into the category of asymmetric algorithms. Also, self-similarity is not self-identity, and the affine transform of shape A will never be exactly identical to shape B. Fractal coding is always lossy.

The mathematics behind the construction of the right affine transforms is quite sophisticated, and for a detailed understanding the reader is referred to the literature [5], [9]. For encoding, an *iterated function system* (IFS) is used. An IFS is a finite set of functions used to look systematically for self-similarity within an input image by scaling, rotating, reflecting, or translating image blocks.

We will try to illustrate the algorithm using an example. Let us assume that we wish to encode a gray-level image of 256×256 pixels. We partition the image into 8×8 pixel blocks R_1, ..., R_{1024}. For the mapping we also define the set of all possible (overlapping) 16×16 pixel blocks as $\{D_j\}$, $j = 1,...,58081$. In the next step, for each R_i we search the D_j that resembles it most. For that purpose we reduce the D_i blocks in the vertical and horizontal dimension by a factor of two so that they have the same size as the R_i blocks. To find the most similar block D_j we allow rotation (by 0, 90, 180 and 270 degrees) and reflection, so we get eight variations for each block D_j. Thus the search requires the computation of a similarity measure for $8 \times 58\,081 = 464\,548$ blocks for each original block R_i. We see why fractal encoding is computationally intensive.

As a similarity measure we can use

$$d_2(\hat{D}_j, R_i) = \sqrt{\sum_{l,m \in \{1,...,8\}} (\hat{d}_{l,m}^{\,j} - r_{l,m}^{\,i})^2}$$

where the $d_{j,l,m}$ and $r_{i,l,m}$ represent the pixel values (gray values) at position l,m in block D_j or R_i respectively.

In addition we can allow the contrast and intensity (luminance) of block D_j to be adjusted to those of the R_i we are trying to match. This corresponds to the minimization of the term

$$\tau_j = \min\left\{ \sum_{l,m \in \{1,...,8\}} (s\hat{d}_{lm}^{\,j} + o - r_{lm}^{\,i})^2 \;\middle|\; s,o \in \Re \right\} \quad j = 1,...,464648$$

The formulas for this minimization are derived in [9]. We will now choose the pixel block D_j with its contrast s_j and intensity o_j that has the smallest value of τ_j (alternatively we could set a threshold parameter below which we would accept a block D_j as being sufficiently similar).

For each block R_i the tuple (R_i,D_j,S_j,o_j) is a mapping w_i of the desired function; the set of $w_i, i=1,...,1024$ is an IFS. For the iterative computation to work, we require $|s_{ji}| < 1$; if that is not the case, we must set s to a value <1. This leads to an artificial quality degradation, but is a requirement for the IFS algorithm to converge. The operator W defined by the IFS $\{w_{ji}\}$, $i=1,...,1024$ is contractive. Thus, if we apply this operator recursively, the image will converge to a fixed point.

Decoding is now quite easy. We start with an arbitrary image and apply W, i.e., the mappings w_{ji}, iteratively to the image. The intermediate versions of the image will converge to a fixed point which closely resembles the original. Notice that we do not transmit any of the pixel values of the original! Only the IFS is transmitted.

Each step in the iterative computation of the image consists of the following operations:

1. reduce the resolution of D_j to the size of R_i
2. rotate and/or reflect the reduced block
3. multiply all pixel values with the contrast s_{ji}
4. add the intensity value o_i to all pixel values of the block
5. store the new intermediate values.

The quality after each iteration can be measured by using the so-called collage theorem, and iteration ends when a predefined quality is reached. It is also possible simply to limit the number of iterations.

Lena image (1:16)   Lena image (1:256)

Figure 4-9: Lena image compressed with fractals (from [9])

Fractal image compression is in fact related to vector quantization, but in contrast to classical vector quantization it uses a vector codebook drawn from the image itself rather than a fixed codebook. We can try to explain the functioning of fractal compression in vector quantization terminology as follows. Images are not stored as a set of quantized transform coefficients, but instead as fixed points of maps on the plane. The codebook is constructed by the encoder from averaged and subsampled isometrics of larger blocks from the image. The encoder determines a self-referencing contraction map of a plane of which the image to be coded is an approximate fixed point. Images are stored by saving the parameters of this map, and decoded by iteratively applying this map to find its fixed point. By effectively storing only the parameters of the contraction map, the compressed version of the image is much smaller than the original.

It is clear that fractal encoders are effective for images composed of isolated straight lines and constant regions since these features are self-similar. In general, for fractal compression to work well, images must be composed of features at a fine scale that are also present at a coarser scale. Fortunately this assumption also holds when more complex features are present because complex image features such as textures tend to possess characteristics that can be exploited by fractal encoders. Pixel values in natural images are far from independent, especially values for pixels that are close together. For some application areas compression ratios can be as high as 1000:1.

As mentioned, fractal image coding is a lossy coding method since natural images are not exactly self-similar. The decoded image is only an approximation of the original, but if the transformations are carefully chosen, the difference between the approximation and the original image is hard to detect at low compression ratios. Figure 4-9 shows a photo of Lena, on the left side compressed to 1:16 of its original size, and on the right side compressed to 1:256.

Image coding with fractals is a relatively new technique. It is used to compress the images for Microsoft's *Encarta*, a multimedia encyclopedia on CD-ROM. A software system for fractal image compression and decompression is available from the company *Iterated Systems*.

4.6 Image Compression with Wavelets

The Fourier or DCT transforms reveal information only about the frequency domain behavior of the image. Since these transforms are based on a linear combination of sine and cosine waves with different coefficients, they are very well suited for homogeneous image regions. In classical Fourier applications (i.e., when coding signals over time), we would say that the representation works well for continuous (repetitive) signals. But in many practical cases we are interested in local specifics of the image (or signal). So the idea is to define a transform based on a linear combination of waveforms that are not periodic but display strong locality. Such waveforms are called *wavelets*.

A wavelet is defined as a set of *basis functions*, derived from the same prototype function. The prototype function is also known as the *mother wavelet.* Two examples of mother wavelets are shown in Figure 4-10. Each of the basis functions has a finite support of a different width, and can be scaled and transformed to meet the requirements of an application. The scaling and transforming coefficients are the equivalent of the Fourier or DCT coefficients; they produce the set of base functions out of the mother wavelet. The different supports allow different trade-offs of time and frequency resolution. To resolve low-frequency details accurately, a wide basis function can be used to examine a large region of the signal, while to resolve time details accurately, a short basis function should be used to examine a small region of the signal.

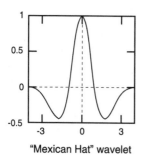
"Mexican Hat" wavelet

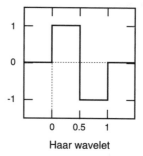
Haar wavelet

Figure 4-10: Two popular mother wavelets

In contrast to DCT-based coding methods which inherently have difficulties with the high-frequency information in the image, wavelet transform coders process the high- and low-frequency parts of the image independently. Most of the energy in the high-frequency portions of images is attributable to edges, both isolated edges and clusters of edges found in textured regions. Not all edges are equally important for the human visual system. Depending on the required compression ratio, more and more information about edges can be removed, thereby degrading image quality.

With the wavelet approach, an image is transformed as a whole; it is not subdivided into pixel blocks, as with DCT-based coding methods. Thus no blocking artifacts occur. Instead, even at high compression ratios, wavelet coders degrade gracefully. The left image in Figure 4-11, compressed to 1:16 of its original size, shows a very good image quality with no visual artifacts. At a compression ratio of 1:256, the right image in Figure 4-11 shows a degraded image quality, but the appearance of the image is quite different from that of DCT-based images or images compressed with fractals.

Lena image (1:16)   Lena image (1:256)

Figure 4-11: An example of artifacts produced by a wavelet transform

Figure 4-12 sows a block diagram of a forward wavelet transform. The image is first filtered along the x dimension, resulting in a low-pass and in a high-pass image. Since the bandwidth of both the low-pass and the high-pass image is now half that of the original image, both filtered images can be down-sampled by a factor of 2 without loss of information. Then both filtered images are again filtered and down-sampled along the y dimension, resulting in four subimages. One of these subimages represents the average signal, and the three remaining images represent the horizontal image features, the vertical features, and the diagonal features.

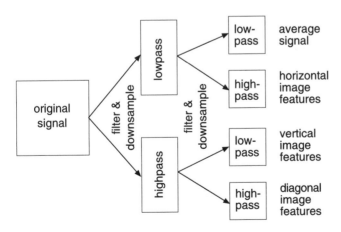

Figure 4-12: Block diagram of the two-dimensional wavelet transform

The average signal, shown on top in the block diagram, is then processed as the new input in the same way. This is repeated recursively until the desired compression ratio is reached.

After the forward wavelet transform, compression has not yet been accomplished. Instead, each application of the forward wavelet transform increases the number of coefficients, i.e., the storage requirement increases. Compression is achieved, as with DCT, by quantizing and entropy encoding the wavelet coefficients. By inverting the coding operations, data can be reconstructed. More information on wavelet transform can be found in [13], [31].

Both DCT and DWT are symmetrical coding methods (unlike compression based on fractals). Due to the better localization of frequencies with DWT, better compression ratios at the same visual quality as with DCT can be achieved. Efficient implementations have been developed for both DCT and DWT, with a small advantage for DCT due to the experience gained in that field; but this might change in the future.

The wavelet-based image compression method described in this section can be extended to compress sequences of digital images by exploiting temporal redundancies in one of two ways. First, standard video compression techniques like hierarchical motion compensation and three-dimensional subband coding can be implemented using wavelets, thereby extending the two-dimensional DWT by the time dimension. Second, instead of performing the complete inverse DWT for each frame in a slowly varying image sequence, only the inverse DWT for those pixels has to be computed that have changed by a meaningful amount between adjacent frames in the sequence. Experiments have shown that higher compression rates can be achieved by the first approach than by the second; but the memory and processor requirements of the first approach are significantly higher than those of the second. For sequences of images much more efficient algorithms can be found, as we will see in the next chapter.

5 Video Compression Techniques

5.1 MPEG-1

The MPEG standard (named after the Moving Picture Experts Group, the ISO committee that created it) defines a bit stream representation for synchronized digital video and audio, compressed to fit into a bandwidth of 1.5 Mbit/s [24], [33]. Interesting details to MPEG can also be found at http://drogo.cselt.stet.it/mpeg/. MPEG-1 consists of three parts, MPEG video, MPEG audio, and MPEG system; the latter is responsible for multiplexing and synchronizing audio and video. About 1.1 Mbit/s are for video, 128 kbit/s for audio, and the remainder for MPEG system packet overhead. The most important application of MPEG-1 is the storage of audio visual information on digital storage media, such as CD-ROM and DAT. When the MPEG standard was developed, the earlier standards H.261 and JPEG were taken into consideration.

MPEG-1 video defines the syntax and semantics of the video bit stream. Like H.261, there are no specifications for the encoder other than to produce a coded bit stream in conformance with the MPEG-1 syntax.

5.1.1 MPEG-1 Blocks and Macroblocks

The MPEG compression algorithm starts with an image in YCbCr format. The basic building block of an MPEG picture is the *macroblock*. It consists of an array of 16×16 luminance (Y) samples and two 8×8 blocks for the two chrominance components (Cb, Cr). The relative position of the chrominance samples between luminance samples is illustrated in Figure 5-1. The 16×16 array of luminance samples is actually decomposed into four 8×8 blocks, to be processed separately. The algorithms described below all operate on one such 8×8 block at a time.

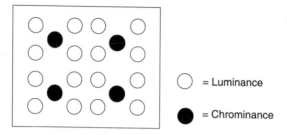

Figure 5-1: Chrominance subsampling

5.1.2   DCT Transformation

Just as in JPEG, the compression of an 8×8 block starts with a Discrete Cosine Transform. The transformation formula is the same as the one used for JPEG. The result is again a matrix of 64 DCT coefficients. The coefficient in the upper left hand corner is called the "DC" coefficient and represents the average gray value (or Cb or Cr color deviation) of the block. The matrix of coefficients is then fed into the quantization step.

5.1.3   Quantization

There is one quantizer step size for the DC coefficient of 8, and 31 possible even-valued quantizer step sizes ranging from 2 to 62 for the AC coefficients. The AC coefficients of inter-coded blocks are quantized with a dead-zone around zero. The quantized values range from –255 to 255. Luminance and chrominance components are quantized using the same quantization table. For more details, see [35] and [40].

5.1.4   Entropy Encoding

Entropy encoding uses run-length-level variable-length coding. If there is no VLC entry for the run-length/level combination, 6-bit escape, 6-bit FLC for run-length, an 8-bit FLC for levels in the range from –127 to 127, and a 16-bit FLC for other levels are used to encode the quantized DCT coefficients.

5.1.5   Frame Types

There are four different frame types in the MPEG-1 standard, namely, I-, P-, B-, and DC frames. The group of picture structure (see Figure 5-2) is not pre-defined in the standard but is one of the optimization possibilities for the encoder. The very first picture of the video stream must be an intra-coded picture (*I-picture*). Beyond the I-picture, there exist three prediction-based or inter-coded picture types. Forward-predicted pictures are also termed *P-pictures*. The reference for these is the last I- or P-picture. Another type of prediction is backward prediction with a reference to a future I- or P-picture (backward prediction is a choice with the interpolation mode, hence assigned to B-pictures). These are completed by the bidirectionally coded frame type (*B-picture*) where the references are the previous and the next I- or P-picture. B-pictures themselves can never be used as a reference. Another picture type is just briefly mentioned here, the *D- or DC-picture* that ignores AC coefficients. It can never be used with the other picture types, and was mainly defined for visible fast-forward or fast-reverse operation where image quality can be much lower, and inter-coded pictures such as P or B cannot be used.

The reference pictures must be transmitted and received before the interpolated pictures can be computed. Therefore, the transmission order and the display order are different. At the beginning, there is always an I-picture. For example, for the first two B-pictures in Figure 5-2, the first I- and the first P-pictures serve as references. The first I-picture is also the reference for this P-picture.

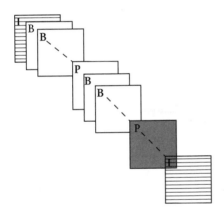

Figure 5-2: MPEG-1 group of pictures

Important aspects for the picture sequence structure in an implementation are time constraints, buffer constraints, necessity of random-access points, or the desired compression/quality trade-off.

5.1.6 Motion-Compensated Prediction

For the P-pictures, MPEG-1 has a *(forward) prediction* mode where a reference frame in the past is used to predict areas of the current frame based on macroblocks (see Table 5-1). The reference frame is not necessarily the preceding frame, but the last I- (intra-coded) or P-frame some time in the past. Furthermore, there is no limitation defined in the MPEG-1 standard for the search area for possible motion vectors.

Table 5-1: Coding Layers of MPEG-1

Video sequence	independent video stream
Group of pictures	random access unit (e.g., IBBPBB)
Picture	single frame in the video sequence
Slice	resynchronization unit, variable number of macroblocks
Macroblock	16×16 Y, 8×8 Cb/Cr (motion compensation)
Block	8×8 pixels (coding unit for DCT)

5.1.7 Motion-Compensated Interpolation

B-pictures use interpolation for even better compression. Interpolation is also termed bidirectional coding, or coding using the average. Like motion-compensated prediction, it utilizes the temporal redundancy among consecutive frames. But while motion-compensated prediction uses only one reference frame (in the past), motion-compensated interpolation makes use of two reference frames, one some time in the past, and one some time in the future (see Figure 5-3).

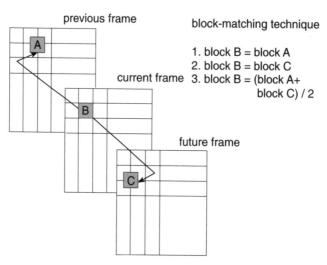

Figure 5-3: Motion-compensated interpolation

For a given target block of the frame currently encoded, the motion estimation algorithm looks for two matching macroblocks, one in the past and the other in the future reference frame. Taking the average of the two reference macroblocks, the prediction error to the target block is calculated. As in motion-compensated prediction, the prediction error and the resulting difference signal are transmitted, applying first DCT, then quantization, and then entropy encoding. But now, there are two motion vectors specifying the coordinate differences to the matching macroblock in the past and in the future reference frame.

The use of the motion estimation process depends on the structure of the video sequence. It is up to the application to determine a picture pattern, that is, the structure of a group of pictures defined by the appearance and order of B- and P-frames between two I-frames. Motion estimation must fulfill its task when B- or P-pictures appear in the picture pattern. This is a very common case, since these achieve the highest degree of compression. The MPEG-1 standard does not specify any limitations for coordinate values of the motion vector. If a P-frame is to be encoded, the motion estimation unit uses the last I- or P-frame as the reference frame, and it tries to find a good match to predict macroblock units of the current frame. If successful, a motion vector and the resulting prediction error are encoded for the macroblock. Otherwise, the macroblock is simply intra-coded. The decision process for B-frames is more complex. Four possibilities must be taken into account: Forward or backward prediction, interpolation, or, if these are not applicable, the macroblock is intra-coded. If interpolation is applied, two reference frames must be available, the closest I- or P-frame in the past and in the future, yielding two motion vectors and one prediction error block. The reference frames for P- and B-pictures must be transmitted first.

By adapting the quantizer, the coding control is able to change the output bit rate, and to improve the picture quality as much as possible.

Figures 5-4 and 5-5 illustrate the overall operation of an MPEG-1 encoder and decoder, respectively.

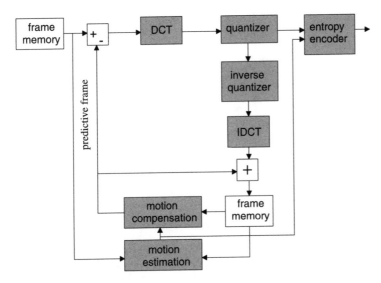

Figure 5-4: MPEG-1 encoder

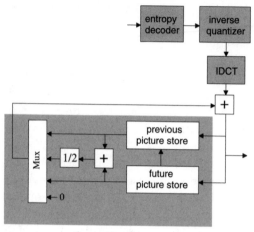

motion compensation

Figure 5-5: MPEG-1 decoder

5.1.8   Image Formats

MPEG-1 processes many different source image formats (sizes). Two standard interchange formats (SIF) are defined, namely PAL (phase alternating line) and NTSC (National Television Standards Committee) (see Table 5-2), in accordance with widely-used European and North American television standards. Restrictions are set by the Constraint Parameter Set (CPS) [35], a set of parameters that should be supported by all decoders. Since an MPEG-1 encoder has so many options to choose from, the Constraint Parameter Set simplifies the implementation of decoders for CPS-conformant streams

Table 5-2: Source image formats of MPEG-1

	Y	Cb/Cr	Frames/s
SIF: PAL	352×288	176×144	25 (50 Hz)
NTSC	352×240	176×120	29.97 (60Hz)

5.1.9   Constraint Parameter Set

The constraint parameter set (CPS) for MPEG-1 defines a set of restrictions the video stream must meet to be regarded as compliant to standard MPEG-1. The purpose of the CPS is to normalize computational complexity, buffer size, and memory bandwidth, and, of course, to assure interoperability between encoders and decoders, especially for hardware implementations. Because of the macro-block restrictions, 396 or 330 per picture, respectively, MPEG-1 video is typically coded at SIF dimensions (352×240 at 30 fps or 352×288 at 25 fps).

Table 5-3 illustrates the parameters of the MPEG-1 Constraint Parameter Set.

Table 5-3: MPEG-1 CPS parameters

horizontal size	<= 720 pixels
vertical size	<= 576 pixels
total number of macroblocks/picture	<= 396
total number of macroblocks/second	<= 396×25 = 330×30
picture rate	<= 30 frames/s
bit rate	<= 1.86 Mbit/s
decoder buffer	<= 376832 bits

5.2   MPEG-2

MPEG-2 is an extension and improvement of the MPEG-1 standard, developed by the same ISO committee. The video part of MPEG-2 permits data rates up to 100 Mbit/s and also supports interlaced video formats and a number of advanced features, including support for HDTV. MPEG-2 video can be used for the digital transmission of video over satellite, cable, and other broadcast channels. It builds upon and improves the completed MPEG-1 standard and has been developed in cooperation with ISO/IEC (IS 13818-2) and ITU (H.262).

Following MPEG-1, the need arose to compress, store, and transmit digital TV broadcast-quality video (ITU-R 601 format). MPEG-1 had some limitations such as the inability to cope with interlaced video and the fact that it was actually optimized for 1.5 Mbit/s. Also, the forthcoming digital video format for High Definition TV (HDTV) called for a new compression standard capable of achieving high compression ratios for large-image high-resolution formats.

MPEG-2 extends the functions provided by MPEG-1 to achieve efficient encoding of audiovisual information at a wide range of resolutions and bit rates, and also to provide full interactive multimedia services such as:

❑ random access for interactive TV,
❑ trick modes that are able to provide VCR-like features such as fast forward, reverse play, slow forward play, etc.,
❑ multiple audio and video flows (stereo, multi-language).

Since MPEG-1 was intended for audiovisual coding for Digital Storage Media (DSM) applications, in particular videos on CD-ROM, and since those are error-free environments, the MPEG-1 Systems part was not designed to be robust to errors. Neither was MPEG-1 intended for transmissions, but for software playback, and thus large variable-length packets were used to minimize overhead.

On the other hand, MPEG-2 targets a variety of multimedia applications, including transmission over lossy channels. The MPEG-2 systems format was designed to improve error resilience, and to carry multiple "programs" simultaneously without requiring them to have a common time base. To be flexible enough, the MPEG-2 system layer defines two types of streams: the *program stream* and the *transport stream*. The former is analogous to the MPEG-1 system stream with a modified syntax and new functions. It provides compatibility with the MPEG-1 system stream, and is intended for software processing with minimal overhead. The latter differs significantly from both the MPEG-1 system stream and the MPEG-2 program stream format. The transport stream uses fixed-length packets of 188 bytes. It is more suited for hardware processing and error correction. Thus, it is well suited for transmission over error-prone channels such as coaxial cable TV networks and packet networks including ATM. The transport stream allows for the multiplexing of multiple programs with independent time bases into a single stream.

Both system streams share a common data structure, the *Packetized Elementary Stream* (PES). PES packets are generated by packetizing the continuous stream of compressed data, either audio or video. A program stream is generated by simply concatenating PES packets with necessary data to generate a single bit stream. A transport stream is obtained by segmenting PES packets into TS packet payloads. A TS packet consists of a 4-byte header followed by 184 bytes of payload.

Originally, the MPEG-2 video specification was primarily intended for coding of interlaced video at standard TV resolution in the range of 4 to 9 Mbit/s. However, the scope of MPEG-2 was widened considerably to include higher resolutions and bit rates as well as hierarchical coding. Among the new features included in MPEG-2 are the support of different chrominance sampling modes. The standard sampling mode used in JPEG, MPEG-1 and H.261 is called (4:2:0); the sampling rates of the two chrominance components are half of the luminance sampling rate; in both the horizontal and the vertical direction (see Figure 5-1). (4:2:2)-sampling produces chrominance components with the same vertical but half the horizontal resolution of the luminance components. This leads to better color quality than (4:2:0). (4:4:4)-sampling is also supported in MPEG-2, which provides identical chrominance and luminance resolutions.

Another new feature of MPEG-2 is scalability. Scalable modes enable video information to be encoded into two or more layers. The standard defines four *layered coding* modes:

❑ *Spatial scalability* allows each frame to be encoded at a range of resolutions that can be built up to the full resolution. This feature could, for example, be used to transmit video simultaneously to standard TV as well as to HDTV terminals.

❑ *Data partitioning* enables the coded data to be separated into high- and low-priority streams. A high-priority stream includes the basic information such as motion vector headers and low-frequency DCT coefficients. The low-priority ones contain the remaining information. This enables multicast filtering, based on the stream priorities.

❑ *Signal-to-noise ratio scalability (SNR)* allows pictures to be encoded in a basic coarse quality version. The enhancement layers providing information required to decode the full quality image.

❑ *Temporal scalability* allows sequence to be encoded a at different frame rates. The base layer will contain the sequence at a low frame rate, and the enhancement layers will contain the remaining frames needed to achieve the full quality.

As with MPEG-1, the MPEG-2 video standard does not specify the video encoding process; instead it specifies the video bit stream syntax and decoding semantics. The basics of MPEG-2 video encoding are the same as for MPEG-1, especially for progressive encoding. In particular, it transforms one digital video signal stream into another (compressed) stream, without understanding the semantics of the objects in the stream. Like MPEG-1, MPEG-2 has four types of pictures: I, P, B, and D. Images are decomposed into macroblocks, consisting of 8×8 blocks. Each block is DCT-transformed, quantized and zig-zag scanned. Motion estimation and compensation are then performed. Finally, entropy encoding is done by applying variable-length coding.

One major difference between MPEG-1 and MPEG-2 lies in MPEG-2's capability to compress interlaced video efficiently. To achieve this, MPEG-2 specifies a choice between two picture structures. Field-pictures consist of fields that are coded independently. With frame-pictures each interlaced field pair is interleaved together into a frame that is then divided into macroblocks and coded. MPEG-2 requires interlaced video to be displayed as alternate top and bottom fields.

Another difference due to interlaced video is the *alternate scan* mode offered by MPEG-2. The zig-zag traversal of the DCT coefficients is the same as in JPEG, and done for the same reason (see Figure 4-6). In frame-pictures, adjacent scan lines come from different fields, and therefore vertical correlation is reduced when there is motion in the scene. The zig-zag scanning may not be optimal in this case. Therefore, the encoder may decide on a picture-by-picture basis which mode is better.

Since MPEG-2 targets a large range of applications, the standard defines a set of profiles and levels that provide different encoding parameters. A profile is a subset of the full MPEG-2 syntax that specifies a particular set of coding features. Each profile is a superset of the preceding profiles. A level specifies a subset of spatial and temporal resolutions which includes a large set of image formats. Table 5-4 summarizes the profiles and levels defined in the standard. The upper bound for the sampling density (pixels/line × lines/frames × frames/s) for each level is also stated. For example, the main profile in the high level has an upper bound of 1920 pixels/line, 1152 lines/frames, and 60 frames/s with a data rate less than or equal to 80 Mbit/s.

The standard does not allow all the profile and level combinations, but only a subset of them. Particular profile and level combinations are designed to support particular classes of applications. The MPEG-2 main profile was defined to support digital video transmission in the range of about 2 to 80 Mbit/s. Parameters of the main profile and the high profile are suitable for supporting HDTV formats. In addition, a hierarchical/scalable profile has been defined to support applications such as compatible terrestrial TV/HDTV, packet-network video systems, and other applications for which multilevel coding is required. In addition, backward compatibility with existing standards (MPEG-1 and H.261) has been defined.

Table 5-4: MPEG-2 video profiles and levels

	Simple profile no B frames not scalable	Main profile B frames not scalable	SNR scalable profile B frames SNR scalable	Spatially scalable profile B frames SNR scalable	High profile B frames spatial or SNR scalable
High level 1920×1152×60		≤ 80 Mbit/s			≤ 100 Mbit/s
High-1440 level 1440×1152×60		≤ 60 Mbit/s		≤ 60 Mbit/s	≤ 80 Mbit/s
Main level 720×576×30	≤ 15 Mbit/s	≤ 15 Mbit/s	≤ 15 Mbit/s		≤ 20 Mbit/s
Low level 352×288×30		≤ 4 Mbit/s	≤ 4 Mbit/s		

The MPEG-2 standard also includes audio compression. Two modes exist: a BC mode backwards compatible with MPEG-1 audio and a new multi-channel mode. The new audio mode specifies the encoding of up to six audio channels;

it is known as the 3/2 mode. This mode specifies the left, center, and right channels plus left and right rear channels. These channels are used for surround sound audio. The sixth channel, which is optional, is a low-frequency enhancement channel. A non-compatible mode able to achieve even better state-of-the-art five-channel audio quality is under consideration.

This concludes our introductory discussion of MPEG-2. For more details the interested reader is referred to the literature. An excellent book is [33].

5.3 MPEG-4

The reader might be surprised that there is no MPEG-3. MPEG-3 was initially planned to be a standard for very high quality video at very high data rates (in particular, HDTV). During early work in the committee it turned out that the new compression algorithms and schemes emerging in MPEG-2 would be appropriate to handle HDTV scenarios. Consequently, MPEG-3 was dropped from the standardization process.

5.3.1 MPEG-4 Overview

MPEG-4 is currently under development by ISO [19]. It is motivated as follows. Multimedia applications are becoming more and more complex. The introduction of virtual reality requires efficient coding of synthetic models. Also, foreseen applications may contain multi-viewpoint scenes and graphics. And interactive applications need compression and encoding scheme different from the TV-like digital *signal* encoding.

The aim of the MPEG-4 working group is to produce a standard that will be efficient, flexible, and extensible in the future. Although the original target of the MPEG-4 committee was the development of a coding standard for very low bit rate applications, the focus has since changed to *object-oriented* video coding.

For example, consider a car driving in front of a city skyline, as shown in Figure 5-6. Instead of coding each image in the clip as a whole, the car in the foreground and the stationary background can be coded independently, with different compression methods or parameter sets. Accompanying audio objects can be identified and coded depending on their contents; examples are background noise, music, and speech. And text appearing in a video could be coded in ASCII and rendered by a parameterized text rendering algorithm on the receiving side.

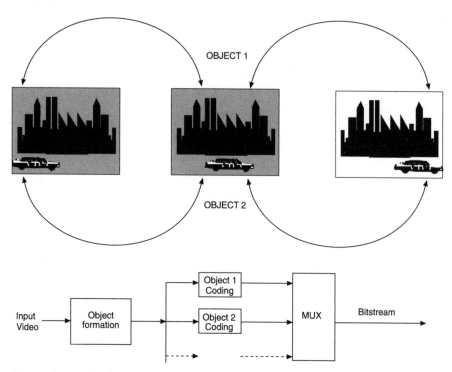

Figure 5-6: Encoding background and foreground as separate objects

The basic functionality classes that the MPEG-4 standard will provide are:

- ❑ Content-based coding and manipulation of multimedia data. This allows interaction with objects in a scene. It also embraces all aspects of data access via the Web browser paradigm.
- ❑ Improved coding efficiency for storage and transmission over heterogeneous networks as well as coding of multiple concurrent streams for multi-viewpoint scenes.
- ❑ Error robustness, in particular for mobile communications.
- ❑ Various scalability modes.

To achieve such capabilities, MPEG-4 has to provide the possibility to access not only pictures but also regions or semantic *objects* within a picture. This leads to the concept of *Video Object Planes* (VOPs). A VOP can be a semantic object that is represented by texture variations and shape information. Each VOP typically contained a single object within a scene. For example, in a video-conference sequence, the head-and-shoulders view of the remote speaker will be contained in one VOP and the background in a second one. The advantage of this architecture is that it allows each object in a sequence of pictures to be coded separately and with a different algorithm. Each algorithm can be chosen to achieve the best quality/compression trade-off for the application.

It is interesting to note that the MPEG-4 standard will not define any specific coding algorithms but rather a method to access tools from which the applications will be able to select and download compression algorithms as required. It is assumed that this structure is flexible enough to allow new coding techniques to be incorporated as new tools into the generic MPEG-4 codec.

The ISO committee motivates the new standard as follows: "For authors, MPEG-4 will enable the production of content that has far greater reusability, has greater flexibility than is possible today with individual technologies such as digital television, animated graphics, World Wide Web (WWW) pages and their extensions. Also, it will be possible to better manage and protect content owner rights. For end users, MPEG-4 will enable many functionalities which could potentially be used on a single compact terminal and higher levels of interaction with content, within the limits set by the author. For all parties involved, MPEG wants to avoid the emergence of a multitude of proprietary, non-interworking formats and players."

5.3.2   Structuring Scenes in MPEG-4

Audiovisual scenes are composed of units of aural, visual, or audiovisual content, called *audio/visual objects* or AVOs . These AVOs can be of natural or synthetic origin; this means they could be captured with a camera or microphone, or generated on a computer. A scene is composed of a number of AVOs. In the following we will illustrate the structuring of a scene using the audiovisual scene depicted in Figure 5-7.

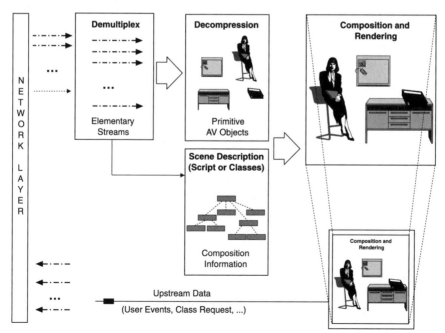

*Figure 5-7: Example of a scene and the components of an MPEG-4 terminal
(adopted from the ISO standard)*

At the leaves of the hierarchy, we find primitive AVOs, such as:

- ❏ a 2-dimensional fixed background,
- ❏ the picture of a talking person (without the background),
- ❏ the voice associated with that person.

MPEG standardizes a number of such primitive AVOs, capable of representing both natural and synthetic content types, which can be either 2D or 3D. In addition to the AVOs mentioned above and shown in Figure 5-7, MPEG-4 defines the coded representation of objects such as:

- ❏ text and graphics,
- ❏ talking heads and associated text to be used at the receiver's end to synthesize the speech and animate the head,
- ❏ animated human bodies.

In their coded form, these objects are represented as efficiently as possible. Examples of such functionalities are error robustness, allowing extraction and editing of an object, or having an object available in a scalable form. It is important to note that in their coded form, objects (aural or visual) can be represented independently of their surroundings or background.

MPEG-4 also provides facilities to describe the composition of a scene from objects. An MPEG-4 scene follows a hierarchical structure which can be represented as a directed acyclic graph. Each node of the graph is an object, as illustrated in Figure 5-8 (note that this graph refers to our example in Figure 5-7). The graph structure is not necessarily static; node attributes (e.g., positioning parameters) can be changed, and nodes can be added, replaced, or removed.

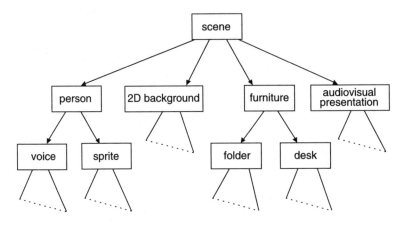

Figure 5-8: Structural description of an MPEG-4 scene

In the MPEG-4 model, audiovisual objects have both a spatial and a temporal extent. Each AV object has a local coordinate system in which the object has a fixed spatiotemporal location and scale. It serves as a handle for manipulating the AV object in space and time. AV objects are positioned in a scene by specifying a coordinate transformation from the object's local coordinate system into a global coordinate system defined by a parent scene description node in the graph.

5.3.3 Multiplexing and Synchronization of Audio-Visual Objects

The MPEG-4 standard specifies an equivalent to the system stream in MPEG-1, or the system and transport streams in MPEG-2. It deals with multiplexing the transmission of objects in transfer.

The *FlexMux* (Flexible Multiplexing) Layer is fully specified by MPEG-4. It contains a multiplexing tool which allows grouping of Elementary Streams (ESs) with a low multiplexing overhead. This may be used, for example, to group ESs with similar QoS requirements.

The *TransMux* (Transport Multiplexing) layer models the layer that offers transport services matching the requested QoS. Only the interface to this layer is specified by MPEG-4. Any suitable existing transport protocol stack such as RTP/UDP/IP, AAL5/ATM, or MPEG-2's transport stream over a suitable link layer may become a specific TransMux instance. The choice is left to the end user or service provider.

5.3.4 Interaction with AVOs

In general, the user observes a scene that is composed following the design of the scene's author. Depending on the degree of freedom allowed by the author, however, the user has the possibility to interact with the scene. Operations a user may be allowed to perform include:

- ❑ Changing the viewing/listening point of the scene, e.g., by navigation through a scene,
- ❑ Dragging objects in the scene to a different position,
- ❑ Triggering an event by clicking on a specific object, e.g. starting or stopping a video stream,
- ❑ Selecting the desired language when multiple language tracks are available.

Streams coming from the network (or a storage device) as TransMux streams are demultiplexed into FlexMux streams and passed to appropriate FlexMux demultiplexers that decompose them into elementary streams. The elementary streams are parsed and passed to the appropriate decoders. Decoding recovers the data in an AV object and performs the necessary operations to reconstruct the original AV object and make it ready for rendering on the appropriate device. Audio and visual objects are represented in their individual coded form.

5.3.5 Coding of Visual Objects

Natural textures, images, and video. The tools for representing natural video in the MPEG-4 visual standard aim at providing standardized core technologies allowing efficient storage, transmission and manipulation of textures, images, and video. These tools will allow the decoding and representation of atomic units of image and video content, called *video objects* (VOs). An example of a VO could be a talking person (without background) which can then be composed with other AVOs (audio-visual objects) to create a scene.

In order to achieve this broad goal the video part of the MPEG-4 standard provides solutions in the form of tools and algorithms for:

- ❏ efficient compression of images and video,
- ❏ efficient compression of textures for texture mapping on 2D and 3D meshes,
- ❏ efficient compression of implicit 2D meshes,
- ❏ efficient compression of time-varying geometry streams that animate meshes,
- ❏ efficient random access to all types of visual objects,
- ❏ extended manipulation functionality for images and video sequences,
- ❏ content-based coding of images and video,
- ❏ content-based scalability of textures, images, and video,
- ❏ spatial, temporal, and quality scalability,
- ❏ error robustness and resilience in error prone environments.

The visual part of the MPEG-4 standard will provide a toolbox with the above.

Synthetic objects. Synthetic objects form a subset of the larger class of computer graphics. The following visual synthetic objects will be described first:

- ❏ Parametric description of a synthetic representation of the human face and body, as well as animation streams of the face and body,
- ❏ Static and dynamic mesh coding with texture mapping,
- ❏ Texture coding for view-dependent applications.

Let us look at facial animation as an example. In MPEG-4 the face is an object with a facial geometry, ready for rendering and animation. The shape, texture, and expressions of the face are generally controlled by the bit stream containing instances of Facial Definition Parameter (FDP) sets and/or Facial Animation Parameter (FAP) sets. Upon construction, the face object contains a generic face with a neutral expression. This face can already be rendered. It is also immediately capable of receiving the FAPs from the bit stream, which will produce animation of the face: expressions, speech, etc.

5.3.6 Coding of Video

Figure 5-9 illustrates the MPEG-4 algorithms to encode rectangular as well as arbitrarily shaped input image sequences. The basic coding structure involves shape coding (for arbitrarily shaped VOs) and motion compensation as well as DCT-based texture coding (using either the standard 8 × 8 DCT of MPEG-2 or a new type of shape-adaptive DCT).

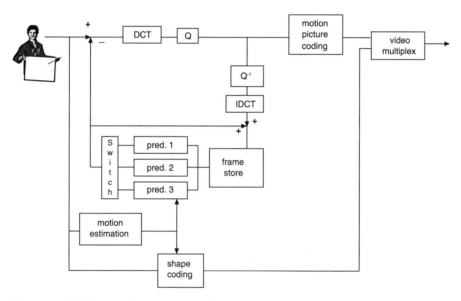

Figure 5-9: MPEG-4 encoder

An important advantage of the content-based coding approach taken by MPEG-4 is that the compression efficiency can be significantly improved for some video sequences by using an appropriate and dedicated object-based motion prediction "tool" for each object in a scene. A number of motion prediction techniques can be used to allow efficient coding and flexible presentation of the objects:

❑ Standard 8 × 8 or 16 × 16 pixel block-based motion estimation and compensation.

❑ Global motion compensation using eight motion parameters that describe an affine transformation.

❑ Global motion compensation based on a static *sprite*. A static sprite is a possibly large still image, describing panoramic background. For each consecutive image in a sequence, only eight global motion parameters describing camera motion are coded to reconstruct the object. These parameters represent the appropriate affine transform of the sprite transmitted in the first frame.

❑ Global motion compensation based on dynamic sprites. Sprites are not transmitted with the first frame but dynamically generated over the scene.

5.3.7   Coding of Textures and Still Images

Efficient coding of visual textures and still images is supported by the visual texture mode of MPEG-4. This mode is based on a special wavelet algorithm that provides very high coding efficiency at a very wide range of bit rates (see Section 4.6). Together with high compression efficiency, the wavelet algorithm also provides spatial and quality scalabilities and also coding of arbitrarily shaped objects.

5.3.8   Scalable Coding of Video Objects

MPEG-4 supports the coding of images and video objects with spatial and temporal scalability, both with conventional rectangular as well as with arbitrary shape. Scalability refers to the ability to decode only a part of a bit stream and reconstruct images or image sequences with:

❑ reduced decoder complexity and thus reduced quality
❑ reduced spatial resolution
❑ reduced temporal resolution
❑ with equal temporal and spatial resolution but with reduced quality.

This functionality is desirable for progressive coding of images and video over heterogeneous networks, as well as for applications where the receiver is not willing or equipped to display the full resolution or full quality images or video sequences. Figure 5-10 illustrates temporal scaling with two video object layers: VOL0 is the base layer, VOL1 the enhancement layer.

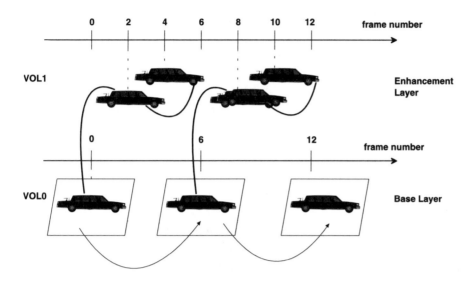

Figure 5-10: Temporal scaling (quality enhancements) in MPEG-4

For the decoding of still images, the MPEG-4 standard will provide spatial scalability with up to eleven levels of granularity. For video sequences a maximum of three levels of granularity will be supported.

MPEG-4 distinguishes three types of decoders to support flexibility and extensibility:

- ❑ A Level 0 (non-programmable) decoder incorporates a pre-specified set of standardized algorithms.
- ❑ A Level 1 (flexible) decoder incorporates a pre-specified set of standardized tools which can be configured into an algorithm in the setup phase.
- ❑ A Level 2 (extensible) decoder provides a mechanism for the encoder to download new tools and algorithms.

5.3.9 MPEG-4 Status

Currently, the MPEG-4 standard is in the verification test phase. MPEG-4 whose ISO/IEC designation will be ISO/IEC 14496, is to be released in November 1998 and will be an International Standard in January 1999.

5.4 MPEG-7

Recently ISO has decided to establish a working group on meta-data, to accompany an audio/video stream on a separate track [19]. The motivation for this work is that there is considerable knowledge on the semantic contents of a video or audio track at the time of production; this knowledge is lost when only the video and audio tracks are stored and/or transmitted. Examples include the names of authors, actors, and directors or the script in a feature film, the names of politicians or celebrities and the exact time of recording in documentaries or newscasts etc. For later access to the digitized material, it would be very desirable to record the meta-knowledge on a separate track with the video and audio.

Figure 5-11 illustrates the scope of the MPEG-7 standard. If we assume that the meta-data is recorded together with the audiovisual data, and synchronization information is available, we can build powerful search engines for finding specific pieces of audio or video in huge digital audiovisual archives or multimedia databases. For example, broadcasting stations could have immediate access to their archive material, and producers of documentaries could easily re-use existing clips for new films.

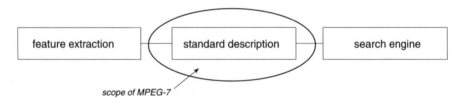

Figure 5-11: Scope of the MPEG-7 Standard

In related research in several laboratories worldwide, video content analysis algorithms are under development, extracting semantic information automatically from video clips [8], [28], [29], [38]. The developers of MPEG-7 imagine the use of such analysis tools to partially automate the process of creating the meta-data.

The role of MPEG-7 as a standard format for meta-data is shown in Figure 5-12.

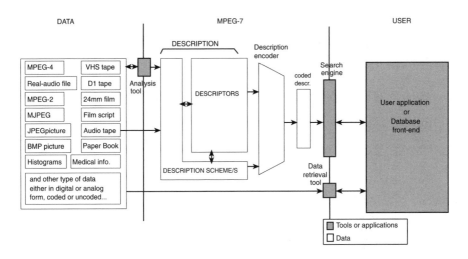

Figure 5-12: Role of MPEG-7 as a standard for meta-data (adopted from the ISO documents)

5.5   H.261

Recommendation H.261 by ITU-T (also called the "p×64 standard") was motivated by the deployment of ISDN (Integrated Services Digital Network). It describes the video coding and decoding methods for the moving picture component of audio visual services at the rate of p×64 kbit/s, where p takes values from 1 to 30, the maximum number of B channels in ISDN (see also [27], [41]). For video telephony, p = 1 or p = 2 is sufficient, better-quality video conferencing needs at least p = 6. Basic rate ISDN, consisting of two B-channels for data and a D-channel for signaling, is available in many countries, enabling video coding at 112 kbit/s and audio at 16 kbit/s to private homes and small offices.

A real-time encoding-decoding system with less than 150 ms delay was the focus of the ITU experts group. H.261 just specifies the syntax and semantics of the coded bit stream, thus allowing the developers of encoders to steadily improve the encoder, or enabling them to choose the trade-offs between performance and cost of their codec. Figure 5-13 shows the block diagram of an H.261 encoder.

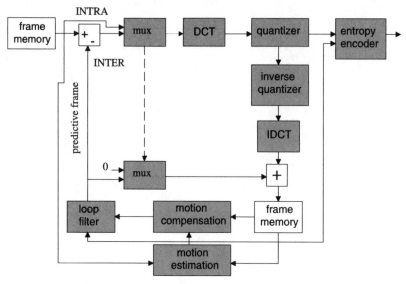

Figure 5-13: H.261 encoder

5.5.1 Quantization

Unlike JPEG and MPEG-1, H.261 does not use quantization matrices; it only applies a quantization *factor*. By changing the quantization step size with a factor common to all coefficients, the codec bit rate can be adapted to the available bandwidth, or to meet the requirements of the hypothetical reference decoder (HRD, see [27], [41]).

In the case of the intra-DC coefficient, there is one quantizer step size (value = 8). For AC coefficients, there are 31 step sizes providing even-valued steps ranging from 2 to 62. There also exists a dead-zone around zero for the AC quantization, meaning that the area that gets quantized to zero is larger than the step size, thus decreasing sensitivity to noise in the input.

5.5.2 Entropy Coding

Unlike JPEG, H.261 represents a number of successive zeroes until the next non-zero value by a hybrid run-length/Huffman encoding. Each run is encoded by a pair (run-length, amplitude). For the most frequent combinations, a variable-length code entry exists. Otherwise, a fixed-length code (20 bits) is used consisting of a 6-bit escape code, 6 bits run-length, and 8 bits for the amplitude.

5.5.3 Motion-Compensated Prediction

The basic concept behind H.261 motion vectors is to look for a certain block of the previous frame that matches very closely an area of the same size in the current frame. If successful, i.e., if a matching block is found, then the differences between the block intensity values (previous and current) and the motion vector (coordinate differences of the corresponding blocks in the x and y directions) are calculated. These differences are also termed *prediction error* because they represent the deviation between the reference block and the predicted block. Usually, a *search area*, a fixed distance in the x and y directions, can be defined to find a match for a block. This is done to reduce the costs of *motion estimation* (process of extracting motion information).

In H.261, the prediction is based on macroblocks (see Table 5-5 for an overview of the H.261 coding layers). A *macroblock* consists of six 8×8 pixel blocks: four luminance blocks and two chrominance blocks, i.e., color subsampling is employed. The four luminance blocks specify a 16×16 pixel area. H.261 takes only the closest previous frame into account for the motion compensation. The motion compensation algorithm tries to find a close match in the previous frame for the macroblock currently encoded. The search area for the motion vector is at most ± 15 pixels in x and y directions. The motion compensation algorithm of H.261 tries to detect motion by checking macroblocks. If it cannot find a close match, it employs exactly the same coding for the macroblocks as in intra-frame coding. Otherwise, the motion vector is coded differentially. Usually, the motion vector of the macroblock to the left of the current block is used as a prediction. Then variable-length coding (VLC) is applied, and it is transmitted along with the DCT-coded prediction error (same process as in intra-frame coding). The motion vector serves as the displacement information for each of the four luminance blocks of a macroblock. For the chrominance blocks, the value of the motion vector is halved in the x and y directions.

Table 5-5: Coding layers of H.261

Picture	one video frame
Group of Blocks	33 macroblocks (1/12 CIF, 1/3 QCIF)
Macroblock	16×16 Y, 8×8 Cb/Cr , motion compensation
Block	8×8 pixels (coding unit for DCT)

5.5.4   Coding Modes

H.261 recognizes two types of video pictures, namely intra-pictures and inter-or predicted pictures. Intra-pictures are coded independently using DCT, quantization, and run-length coding. Beyond this, H.261 tries to make use of temporal redundancy between frames by motion-compensated prediction. If the motion estimation is successful, and the prediction error is not too large, inter-frame coding is applied for the macroblocks.

5.5.5   Coding Algorithm

An H.261 encoder processes image files in CIF (Common Intermediate Format) or QCIF (Quarter CIF), see Table 5-6. The first frame to be transmitted is always an intra-coded frame. The image is coded blockwise. That is, the entire picture is divided into non-overlapping 8×8 pixel blocks on which, first, the DCT is applied. The resulting 64 DCT coefficients are quantized and reordered in a zig-zag fashion. Finally, entropy coding is employed on the coefficients. For the purpose of inter-frame coding, the most recent frame is decoded again within the encoder, using inverse quantization and inverse DCT (IDCT). This is done in order to obtain exactly the same reference frame as the decoder.

For the next frame to be encoded, the previously coded frame is used for making the decision about intra- or inter-frame coding of the macroblock. The motion estimation process can result in four possible decisions for the coding of a macroblock:

1. Intra-coding where the original intensity values are transform coded.
2. Inter-coding without motion compensation. That is, the motion vector has the value zero. Therefore, just the prediction error (difference in intensity values) is transmitted.
3. Inter-coding with motion compensation and non-zero motion vector.
4. Beyond motion compensation, a filter can be used to smooth the picture (to improve the image quality), which is especially useful for low bit rates.

Besides the coding of a macroblock, there is also the possibility of skipping a macroblock. Therefore, the six blocks of a macroblock are examined. If all or nearly all quantized sample values of a block are zero, it may not be encoded at all. If it is the same for all six blocks of a macroblock to be inter-coded without motion compensation, the whole macroblock may be skipped [35]. It is even possible to skip up to three frames between two coded frames, but at least once in every 132 transmitted frames a macroblock must be intra-coded to alleviate error propagation (forced updating, later also adopted by MPEG-1).

Table 5-6: Source image formats of H.261

	CIF	QCIF
Y	352×288	176×144
Cb, Cr	176×144	88×72

As the reader has probably noticed, there are many similarities between MPEG-1 and H.261. Both standards were developed at about the same time. A major difference between MPEG-1 and H.261 is the way H.261 takes care of motion information between consecutive frames: Whereas MPEG-1 specifies a picture pattern (group of pictures), H.261 attempts to predict the current picture from only the previous one, i.e., there is no bidirectional interpolation. This is due to the strict timing requirements of online applications (video telephony, video conferencing). In contrast, MPEG-1 was originally developed for video on CD-ROM, i.e., for a very different application scenario. Another difference is the fact that H.261 does not use spectral quantization, i.e., the quantization factor is the same for all DCT coefficients.

5.6   H.263

The development of modems allowing transmission in the range of 28 to 33 kbps over telephone networks paved the way for the development of an improved version of H.261 for conversational video services at very low bit rates. In 1996 ITU-T released the H.263 standard. H.263 is an enhanced version of H.261 that achieves higher coding efficiency. A possible application is the transmission of an A/V data stream over a V.34 modem connection, using 20 kbit/s for video and 6.5 kbits for audio. Like H.261, H.263 is a video coding standard; it does not specify audio or systems multiplexing, which are defined in related ITU-T standards.

Although H.263 was initially designed for low bit rates, this limitation has now been removed. It is expected that the standard will be used for a wide range of bit rates. H.263 has the potential to replace H.261 in most applications.

H.263 is one of the best methods available today when it comes to video compression efficiency. The coding algorithm of H.263 is similar to that used by H.261, but with some improvements and changes to improve performance and error recovery:

❏ Half-pixel precision is used for motion compensation whereas H.261 used full pixel precision and a loop filter. In other words, the unit for motion vectors is half a pixel rather than a pixel.

❏ Some parts of the hierarchical structure of the data stream are now optional, so the codec can be configured either for a lower data rate or for better error recovery.

❏ There are now four optional, negotiable options included to improve performance. Unrestricted motion vectors allow references that are outside the picture (edge samples being duplicated); this can lead to larger motion vectors. Syntax-based arithmetic coding can replace the standard variable-length code for even better efficiency. Advanced prediction computes a motion vector for each 8×8 luminance block for P-frames. And forward and backward frame interpolation similar to MPEG can be supported: a PB-frame codes two pictures as one unit, with a P computed from the previous reference frame, immediately followed by a B interpolated between the two P's. Using the advanced negotiable options in H.263, one can often achieve the same quality as H.261 with less than half the number of bits.

❏ H.263 supports five resolutions. In addition to QCIF and CIF there is SQCIF, 4CIF, and 16CIF. SQCIF is approximately half the resolution of QCIF, 4CIF and 16CIF are 4 and 16 times the resolution of CIF, respectively (see Table 5-7). The 4CIF and 16CIF resolutions compete with other higher bit rate video coding standards such as MPEG-2.

To summarize, recommendation H.263 is an improvement of H.261 and takes into account the experience gained with the MPEG video standards.

Table 5-7: Image formats in H.263

Picture Format	Luminance Pixels	Luminance Lines	H.261 Support	H.263 support	Uncompressed bitrate (Mbit/s)			
SQCIF	128	96		YES	1.0	1.5	3.0	4.4
QCIF	176	144	YES	YES	2.0	3.0	6.1	9.1
CIF	352	288	Optional	Optional	8.1	12.2	24.3	36.5
4CIF	704	576		Optional	32.4	48.7	97.3	146.0
16CIF	1408	1152		Optional	129.8	194.6	389.3	583.9

5.7   H.263 versus MPEG-1 and MPEG-2

H.263 uses the same luminance/chrominance color space as H.261 and MPEG-1: the chrominance is always half the number of samples in the horizontal and vertical directions (4:2:0). The macroblock and block definitions are also the same as those of MPEG-1 and H.261, and the DCT equations are the same. Decoders must have motion compensation capability [33]. H.263 (similar to H.261) supports only predefined picture sizes, unlike the MPEG standards. The unit for motion vectors is half a pixel for better precision, like in MPEG-2, but unlike in H.261 and MPEG-1. Another difference concerns the negotiable options in H.263: H.263 has overlapped block motion compensation, motion vectors outside the picture, and syntax-based arithmetic coding. These options are not found in MPEG-1 or MPEG-2.

H.263 is often better than MPEG-1/MPEG-2 for low resolutions and low bit rates. It is a superset of H.261, and provides better quality at lower bit rates.

5.8   H.320 and T.120: ITU-T's New Families of Videoconferencing Standards

The ITU-T H.320 and T.120 series of standards comprise the core technologies for multimedia teleconferencing [20]. The H.320 series defines videoconferencing data streams over different types of networks. The T.120 standards address real-time data conferencing, with an emphasis on data transmission and management of multipoint sessions. By the end of 1996, a version of each standard was ratified by the ITU.

5.8.1   H.320 Overview

The H.320 series governs the basic videotelephony concepts of audio, video and graphical communications by specifying requirements for processing audio and video information, providing common formats for compatible audio/video inputs and outputs.

The H.320 standard includes many options that may be included in a videoconferencing system. It supports different formats of video resolution, and also three different audio algorithms, each providing different levels of quality and bandwidth consumption. Various frame rates can be selected, up to 30 frames per second. Also, additional processing when encoding the video can be selected to improve the quality. Further, it supports the T.120 standard that includes many specifications for document conferencing.

H.321 is the standard developed for networks using ATM and broadband ISDN. H.322 is a standard developed for videoconferencing over a LAN with a fixed bandwidth. There is a separate channel used for time-dependent voice and audio transmission. H.323 is a standard for videoconferencing over a LAN that uses either Ethernet or Token Ring. Finally, H.324 is the standard developed for videoconferencing over an analog telephone network. Table 5-8 summarizes the family of standards.

Table 5-8: Overview of the H.320 family of recommendations

	H.320 Narrow-band VTC	H.324 Low Bitrate VTC	H.322 Iso-Ethernet VTC	H.323 Ethernet VTC	H.321 ATM VTC	H.310 High Res ATM VTC
Video	H.261	H.261 H.263	H.261	H.261 H.263	H.261	MPEG-2 H.261
Audio	G.711 G.722 G.728	G.723	G.711 G.722 G.723 G.728	G.711 G.722 G.723 G.728 G.729	G.711 G.722 G.728	MPEG-1 MPEG-2 G.7xx
Data	T.120	T.120 T.434 T.84 Others	T.120	T.120	T.120 H.281 (H.224)	T.120
Multiples	H.221	H.223	H.221	H.22z	H.221	H.222.1 H.221
Signaling	H.230 H.242	H.245	H.230 H.242	H.230 H.245	H.230 H.242	H.245
Multi-point	H.243	N/A	H.243	N/A	H.243	N/A
Encryption	(In draft revision) H.233 H.234	H.233 (adapted in H.324) H.234	(By reference to H.320)	TBD	H.233 H.234	N/A

Let us take a look at H.323 for videotelephony over LANs as an example. The H.323 standard is an extension of H.320, which addressed videoconferencing over ISDN and other circuit switched networks and services. Since H.320 was ratified in 1990, corporations have increasingly implemented Local Area Networks (LANs) and LAN gateways to a Wide Area Network (WAN). H.323 is a logical and necessary extension of the H.320 standard to include corporate intranets and packet-switched networks generally. Because it is based on the Real-Time Protocol (RTP/RTCP) from the IETF, H.323 can also be applied to video over the Internet.

With the ratification of these core components, and the range of networks H.323 can be applied to, products and services based on H.323 are beginning to appear.

Audio is another important component of a videoconferencing system whose main purpose is for speech. The standards provide mainly telephone quality audio over different data rates depending on the type of underlying network. H.320 videoconferencing using ISDN supports three of these, including G.711, G.722, and G.728. H.324 videoconferencing using POTS ("plain old telephone service") supports a different audio standard called G.723. These are also contained in Table 5-8.

5.8.2 T.120 Overview

The T.120 standards cover the *document conferencing* (data sharing) portion of a multimedia teleconference. The recommendations specify how to efficiently and reliably distribute files and graphical information in real-time during a multi-point multimedia meeting. The objective is to assure interoperability between terminals without either participant assuming prior knowledge of the other system; permit data sharing among participants in a multimedia tele-conference, including white board image sharing, graphic display information, and image exchange; and specify infrastructure protocols for audiographic or audiovisual applications.

The T.120 series governs the audiographic portion of the H.320, H.323, and H.324 series and operates either within these or by itself. The T.120 suite consists of a series of recommendations, which are summarized, along with their current ITU status below.

The T.120 family of standards comprises the following recommendations:

- ❑ T.120 – Transmission Protocols for Multimedia Data
- ❑ T.121 – Generic Application Template
- ❑ T.122 – Multipoint Communication Service for Audiographics Con-ferencing
- ❑ T.123 – Protocol Stacks for Audiographic Teleconferencing
- ❑ T.124 – Generic Conference Control
- ❑ T.125 – Multipoint Communication Service Protocol Specification
- ❑ T.126 – Multipoint Still Image and Annotation Protocol
- ❑ T.127 – Multipoint Binary File Transfer
- ❑ T.128 – Audio Visual Control for Multipoint Multimedia Systems.

The T.120 protocol can be included in a H.32x videoconferencing system as the data component, or it can be used alone for data conferencing without video. The standard supports multipoint videoconferencing. It can enable users to share documents and interact with them in real time. Electronic whiteboarding can be done as well as multipoint file transfers.

The T.120 standard contains a series of communication and application protocols and services that provide support for real-time, multi-point data communications. These multipoint facilities are important building blocks for a whole new range of collaborative applications, including desktop data confer-encing, multi-user applications, and multiplayer gaming.

Multi-point Data Delivery. T.120 provides an elegant abstraction for developers to create and manage a multi-point domain with ease. From an application per-spective, data is seamlessly delivered to multiple parties in "realtime".

Interoperability. T.120 allows endpoint applications from multiple vendors to interoperate. T.120 also specifies how applications may interoperate with (or through) a variety of network bridging products and services that also support the T.120 standard.

Reliable Data Delivery. Error-corrected data delivery ensures that all endpoints will receive each data transmission.

Multicast Data Delivery. In multicast enabled networks, T.120 can employ reliable (ordered, guaranteed) and unreliable delivery services. Unreliable data delivery is also available without multicast. By using multicast, the T.120 infrastructure reduces network congestion and improves performance for the end user. The T.120 infrastructure can use both unicast and multicast simultaneously, providing a flexible solution for mixed unicast and multicast networks. The Multicast Adaptation Protocol (MAP) is expected to be ratified in early 1998.

Network Transparency. Applications are completely shielded from the underlying data transport mechanism being used. Whether the transport is a high-speed LAN or a simple dial-up modem, the application developer is only concerned with a single, consistent set of application services.

Application Independence. Although the driving market force behind T.120 was teleconferencing, its designers purposely sought to satisfy a much broader range of application needs. Today, T.120 provides a generic, real-time communications facility that can be used by many different applications. These applications include interactive gaming, virtual reality and simulations, real-time subscription news feeds, and process control applications.

Scalability. T.120 is defined to be easily scalable from simple PC-based architectures to complex multiprocessor environments characterized by their high performance. Resources for T.120 applications are plentiful, with practical limits imposed only by the confines of the specific platform running the software.

Co-existence with other Standards. T.120 was designed to work alone or within the larger context of other ITU standards, such as the H.32x family of video conferencing standards. T.120 also supports and cross-references other important ITU standards, such as the V.series modem.

5.8.3 Tranport Stacks – T.123

T.120 applications expect the underlying transport to provide reliable delivery of its Protocol Data Units (PDUs) and to segment and sequence that data. T.123 specifies transport profiles for each of the following:

- ❑ Public Switched Telephone Networks (PSTN)
- ❑ Integrated Services Digital Networks (ISDN)
- ❑ Circuit Switched Digital Networks (CSDN)

- ❏ Packet Switched Digital Networks (PSDN)
- ❏ TCP/IP
- ❏ Novell Netware IPX (via reference profile).

5.8.4   Multipoint Communication Service (MCS) – T.122, T.125

T.122 defines the multi-point services available to the developer, while T.125 specifies the data transmission protocol. Together they form MCS, the multi-point "engine" of the T.120 conference. MCS relies on T.123 to deliver the data. (Use of MCS is entirely independent of the actual T.123 transport stack(s) loaded.) MCS is a powerful tool that can be used to solve virtually any multi-point application design requirement. MCS is an elegant abstraction of a complex organism. Learning to use MCS effectively is the key to successfully developing real-time applications.

In a conference, multiple endpoints (or MCS nodes) are logically connected together to form what T.120 refers to as a domain. Domains generally equate to the concept of a conference. An application may actually be attached to multiple domains simultaneously. For example, the chairperson of a large online conference may simultaneously monitor information being discussed among several activity groups.

In a T.120 conference, nodes connect upward to a Multipoint Control Unit (MCU). The MCU model in T.120 provides a reliable approach that works in both public and private networks. Multiple MCUs may be easily chained together in a single domain.

5.8.5   Generic Conference Control (GCC) – T.124

Generic Conference Control provides a comprehensive set of facilities for establishing and managing the multipoint conference. It is with GCC that we first see features that are specific to the electronic conference.

At the heart of GCC is an important information base about the state of the various conferences it may be servicing. One node, which may be the MCU itself, serves as the Top Provider for GCC information. Any actions or requests from lower GCC nodes ultimately filter up to this Top Provider.

Using mechanisms in GCC, applications create conferences, join conferences, and invite others to conferences. As endpoints join and leave conferences, the information base in GCC is updated and can be used to automatically notify all endpoints when these actions occur. GCC also knows who is the Top Provider for the conference. However, GCC does not contain detailed topological information about the means by which nodes from lower branches are connected to the conference.

Every application in a conference must register its unique application key with GCC. This enables any subsequent joining nodes to find compatible applications. Furthermore, GCC provides robust facilities for applications to exchange capabilities and arbitrate feature sets. In this way, applications from different vendors can readily establish whether or not they can interoperate and at what feature level. This arbitration facility is the mechanism used to ensure backward compatibility between different versions of the same application.

5.8.6   Multipoint Binary File Transfer – T.127

T.127 specifies a means for applications to transmit files between multiple endpoints in a conference. Files can be transferred to all participants in the conference or to a specified subset of the conference. Multiple file transfer operations may occur simultaneously in any given conference and developers can specify priority levels for the file delivery. Finally, T.127 provides options for compressing files before delivering the data.

6   Quality and Performance: Experimental Results

The reader should now be familiar with the basic compression algorithms for video, lossless and lossy, as well as with the composite schemes used in the most important international standards. As we have seen, the algorithms are controlled by a number of parameters, such as the quantization step size, the range of motion vector searches, Huffman tables, etc. These were built into the standards in order to adapt the algorithms to the different needs of the applications, e.g., medical versus entertainment.

In practice, the right choice of these parameters is of crucial importance: It influences the temporal performance of the algorithms, the bit rate of the compressed stream (or disk space for storage), and the visual quality. However, there are no general hints or rules for an optimal choice of these parameters. This chapter analyzes the effect of the various parameters and attempts to give advice as to how they should be set for a specific application environment.

6.1   Measures of Quality and Performance

It is important to establish measures for quality and performance before we can discuss the effect of the parameters in detail. For visual quality, this is quite difficult. Lossy compression schemes will deliver an image or video clip to the receiver which is deteriorated compared to the original. The question is: Exactly how bad is it?

6.1.1   Measures of Visual Quality

We would like to characterize the visual quality of an image or a video with one characteristic parameter, or a small set of parameters. Intuitively, we think of "sharpness," of "color preservation," etc. Unfortunately, there is no good physical measure for these. For example, a high pixel resolution does not guarantee a sharp image; it is a prerequisite, but compression and decompression can destroy sharp edges that were visible in the original, at the same resolution. The perception of visual quality is based on the very complex system of the human eye, and it is subjective.

One possible solution of the problem is to show a series of images or video clips to a large number of people and evaluate their subjective impressions statistically. This was done for synchronization properties of multiple multimedia data streams at IBM's European Networking Center in Heidelberg [44], and in many other cases in television research and in digital image research. But for our large and complex set of parameters, this would be very costly and time-consuming. We must attempt to define a quality measure that can be computed automatically for our experiments.

For still images, we will use the Signal-to-Noise Ratio (SNR). This is a measure used very widely in analog electronics. It describes the energy of the pure, undistorted signal in relation to the (unavoidable) noise existing in all real systems. In our context, we will compare the final image, after compression and decompression, with the original. We call the difference between the two *noise*. We can then define the signal-to-noise ratio for gray-scale images as follows:

$$SNR := 10 \times \log_{10} \times \left(\frac{\sum_{i=1}^{M} \sum_{j=1}^{N} \left(F_{i,j}^{\text{orig}} \right)^2}{\sum_{i=1}^{M} \sum_{j=1}^{N} \left(F_{i,j}^{\text{orig}} - F_{i,j}^{\text{decomp}} \right)^2} \right)$$

with F^{orig} = Y component of the original and
F^{decomp} = Y component of the decompressed image.
The signal-to-noise ratio is measured in decibel (dB).

For video clips, we use a visual quality measure which we call Q_v. It is based on recent results from the literature [51]. The definition of Q_v for our experimental results is the subject of Section 6.6.

In a series of experiments the authors of [51] validated this measure with human users. They found that the subjective impression of visual quality of video clips corresponded very well with the computed values for Q_v. Other researchers have proposed other measures for visual quality (e.g., [49]), and there are no reports yet on their relative performance. We arbitrarily chose the measure from [51].

6.1.2 Measures of Performance

Performance measures are much easier to determine. The most relevant ones for compression algorithms are obviously

- ❏ the compression ratio R,
- ❏ the compression time T_{comp}, and
- ❏ the decompression time T_{decomp}.

The compression ratio R is defined as

$$R = \frac{S_{comp}}{S_{orig}}$$

where S_{orig} is the size of the original image or clip, and S_{comp} is the size of the compressed image or clip. In this chapter, S_{orig} is computed as follows:

$$S_{orig} = 352 \times 288 \times 1.5 \text{ [bytes]}$$

The assumed YUV file size per frame based on the CIF format is calculated by the product of the image resolution (352×288) and a factor representing the luminance-chrominance color space. Converting from RGB to YUV yields a reduction in data of 2 to 1 (color subsampling). Thus, instead of 3 bytes per pixel in RGB format, just 1.5 bytes per pixel are needed in YUV format.

The compression and decompression times obviously depend on the hardware/software environment. Since we are only interested in the *relative* performance of the algorithms, based on the choice of parameters, this influence is factored out in our experiments. We have used a profiling tool to record the number of machine instructions executed within the encoder/decoder subroutines. Dividing this number by the clock rate of the CPU yields a time value for a particular machine which we use in our comparisons.

Note that T_{comp} and T_{decomp} are not necessarily the same. In many algorithms the compression time is much longer than the decompression time. For example, when motion compensation is used in MPEG, the compression step must search for a best match between the current macroblock and the reference frame. Depending on the search range, this can be a very time-consuming operation. The result are motion vectors indicating the repositioning of the old macroblock in the new frame. The decompression step simply repeats the old macroblock, perhaps slightly modified according to the delta values, in a new pixel position; this is much faster than the search, and thus $T_{comp} > T_{decomp}$.

As mentioned earlier, compression algorithms where $T_{decomp} \neq T_{comp}$ are called *asymmetric*. They can be very useful if an image or a video stream is compressed only once and decompressed many times, e.g., in video-on-demand applications.

6.2 Experimental Setup

For a thorough evaluation of the effect of control parameters in the compression algorithms, we conducted a series of experiments. With a series of still images and video clips, we ran the standardized algorithms JPEG, MPEG-1, and H.261 with various parameter settings and observed the resulting quality and performance. At the time of the experiments, we did not have an MPEG-2 or an

H.263 encoder/decoder available, but, as explained in Chapter 5, the basic algorithms used in these newer compression standards are very similar to those in JPEG, MPEG-1, and H.261. Since we are only interested in understanding the principles of video compression, our experiments are sufficient.

6.2.1   Image and Video Material

For our experiments, we took pictures and video clips from outdoor scenes in the city of Mannheim. A first series of images and video clips was taken at the palace ("Schloß") in Mannheim. Here the emphasis is on structure, in particular lines and edges. An original uncompressed still image is shown in Figure 6-1.

Figure 6-1: Original image of palace

A second series of images and video clips was shot with an emphasis on colors. They were taken at a park in Mannheim and show flowers. An original uncompressed still image is shown in Figure 6-2.

Figure 6-2: Original image of flowers

A third series of video clips was taken at the local farmers' market. We used a high-end PAL consumer video camera. Here, the emphasis was on a colorful, fine-grain image with motion. An original uncompressed still image from that video clip is shown in Figure 6-3.

Figure 6-3: Original image from the market video clip

A fourth series of video clips was taken at a park in Mannheim. This series is an example for video panning across a colorful image. Characteristic for this video is the transition from the first part dominated by flowers to the middle section with an increasing lawn area, and back to the flowers. An original still image from the clip is shown in Figure 6-4.

Figure 6-4: Original image from the flowers video clip

6.2.2 Digitization

The original still images were digitized on a PC with a miroVIDEO DC20 frame grabber board. The result was an AVI file of still images of 360×270 pixels. The resolution was then scaled to the CIF resolution of 352×288 pixels which was used as the input format for the experiments. All originals were stored on disk, and are included on the CD-ROM accompanying this book.

The original videos were also digitized on the PC, and for comparison on a Silicon Graphics Indigo II workstation, using the Galileo Video Digitizer Board and the Cosmo Compression Board. In our laboratory, it was not possible to grab video at the full frame rate of 30 or 25 frames/s and store the digital frames on disk in uncompressed format. Rather, a hardware JPEG compression step followed the frame grabbing immediately, on all our equipment. Software tools were then used to convert the resulting series of high-quality JPEG images into an MPEG-1 or H.261 data stream. We are aware of the fact that artifacts can be introduced by the unavoidable JPEG compression following digitization. However, the highest possible compression quality was chosen here, and we had no alternative.

6.2.3 Compression

For our JPEG experiments, we used the software codec from PVRG (Portable Video Research Group at Stanford University, [39]). The DCT step of this codec allows, in conformance with the JPEG standard, a separate quantization factor to be set for each DCT coefficient; in other words, a quantization table with 64 entries is provided. The quantization values for luminance and chrominance were set by the codec developers and are shown in Tables 6-1 and 6-2. These default quantization table entries are the result of image quality measurements [32].

The quantization table entry precision is either 8 or 12 bits, depending on the sample precision of the components in the frame. The standard defines 8-bit sample precision for the JPEG baseline method, and it should be the same for the quantization. These values are used for our tests.

Table 6-1: Luminance quantization for an 8x8 DCT block

16	11	10	16	24	40	51	61
12	12	14	19	26	58	60	55
14	13	16	24	40	57	69	56
14	17	22	29	51	87	80	62
18	22	37	56	68	109	103	77
24	35	55	64	81	104	113	92
49	64	78	87	103	121	120	101
72	92	95	98	112	100	103	99

Table 6-2: Chrominance quantization for an 8x8 DCT block

17	18	24	47	99	99	99	99
18	21	26	66	99	99	99	99
24	26	56	99	99	99	99	99
47	66	99	99	99	99	99	99
99	99	99	99	99	99	99	99
99	99	99	99	99	99	99	99
99	99	99	99	99	99	99	99
99	99	99	99	99	99	99	99

In addition, this codec allows a global quantization factor to be set and applied to all DCT coefficients. This is a special feature of this codec, not of the JPEG standard. The real quantization value for each coefficient is thus the product of the global factor and the individual quantization table entry. For our experimental comparisons, we left the quantization table unchanged, but set the global quantization factor to 1, 6, 12, and 20. The results with these quantization factors are shown below.

6.2.4 Decompression

Decompression was done with the same software codec from PVRG. The decompressed images were stored on disk for later evaluation.

6.2.5 Display

For the best possible visual precision, the workstations used in our experiments had true-color displays, i.e., the monitors accepted 24 bits per pixel in RGB representation. Many PCs and workstations are only equipped with 8-bit graphics; our experience shows that the conversion of high-quality images to color-lookup-table technology distorts colors considerably.

6.2.6 Post-Production for the CD-ROM

This entire chapter is available in HTML format on the CD-ROM accompanying this book. We also provide the reader with the possibility to view most of our compressed file outputs. The HTML file contains links to compressed files. The following compressed output formats are provided:

- ❏ JPEG
- ❏ MPEG

The results of our still-image compression experiments are stored on the CD-ROM in JPEG format. Those files should be displayable by every HTML browser with an integrated JPEG viewer. For our video compression experiments, we provide the compressed MPEG-1 video clips. To view those files the reader must have an MPEG-1 player installed. Unfortunately, we are unable to present the uncompressed images and/or videos on the CD-ROM because there is no standard image format for 24-bit graphics in browsers. Also, many readers will not have high-resolution 24-bit graphics displays on their machines. So it is not possible to compare the visual quality of the compressed images and videos with the uncompressed originals.

6.3   Experiments with JPEG Still Image Compression

The most important parameter in the JPEG algorithm is the quantization step size. As we have explained earlier, quantization is performed after the DCT transformation; it assigns a fixed number of distinct values to the amplitude range. The higher the quantization step size, the fewer different values we can encode, the fewer bits we need per value, and the higher is the loss in precision. As explained above, the actual quantization step size of the PVRG codec we used is the table value multiplied by the global factor.

Let us now first look at the series of palace images. In each of our series, the first image is the original (Fig. 6-5), the others are those obtained after compression and decompression. We also list our quality measures with each decompressed image, namely the SNR value and the performance measures.

6.3.1   Series 1: The Palace

We use our palace image to illustrate the compression effects on sharp edges. Figures 6-6 to 6-9 depict the experimental results (see also Appendix 7.1).

Figure 6-5: JPEG palace original image

Figure 6-6: JPEG palace image with global q-factor 1

SNR [dB]	21.07
R [%]	10.78
T_{comp} [s]	0.283
T_{decomp} [s]	0.283

Figure 6-7: JPEG palace image with global q-factor 6

SNR [dB]	19.24
R [%]	4.04
T_{comp} [s]	0.267
T_{decomp} [s]	0.267

Figure 6-8: JPEG palace image with global q-factor 12

SNR [dB]	17.68
R [%]	2.76
T_{comp} [s]	0.267
T_{decomp} [s]	0.233

Figure 6-9: JPEG palace image with global q-factor 20

SNR [dB]	16.73
R [%]	2.27
T_{comp} [s]	0.250
T_{decomp} [s]	0.233

In the first two figures of compressed images we see almost no difference in quality. The quantization loss is negligible, but the compression ratio is fairly low (R = 10.78% and 4.04%). In the last two figures we see severe blocking artifacts all over the image. The basic JPEG block size of 8 × 8 pixels is clearly visible.

In the intermediate examples, we observe behavior which is characteristic for JPEG. When the colors within one 8 × 8 block are all nearly the same so that they all fall into the same quantization interval, the only component encoded in the data stream is the DC value, i.e., the upper left corner of the matrix. All AC components are so close to the DC component that they fall into the zero quantization interval. Subsequent run-length coding finds long stretches of zeroes, leading to a high compression ratio. These blocks will be monochrome after decompression.

On the other hand, if a block has sufficient color variation to have AC components in different quantization intervals, the decompressed block has more detail in its colors. The higher we choose the quantization step size, the more monochrome blocks we can identify.

If we take a closer look at the image in Figure 6-8 (q-factor 12), we can see more interesting details. As we have explained earlier, the second DCT matrix element in the first row (c_{12}) corresponds to a low AC frequency. It can be visualized by four horizontal stripes. If we take a close look, we can identify several blocks in the image where we see exactly this pattern. If we print out the DCT matrix for this example we see that only the coefficients c_{11} and c_{12} exist for this 8×8 block, all others are zero. Similarly, we can find other blocks in the image where only c_{11} and c_{21} are greater than zero, leading to four vertical stripes in the decompressed block.

The palace image has many clear lines and edges, and so the increase in quantization step size leads to clearly visible effects quickly. Remember that high frequencies are important to represent sharp edges in the image. The deteriorating visual quality can also be derived from the worsening SNR values. With a quantization factor of 1, we have measured a SNR value of 21.07 dB. When we increased the quantization factor, that SNR value degraded to 16.73 dB.

Figure 6-10 summarizes the change of compression ratio and compression and decompression times caused by increasing quantization factors.

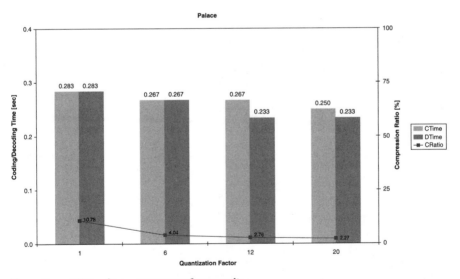

Figure 6-10: JPEG palace – summary of our results

6.3.2 Series 2: The Flowers

In contrast to the palace series, the *flower* images have no sharp edges, so we can expect that the effect of quantization will not be as visually disturbing. Again, in our series of images the first one is the original (Fig. 6-11), followed by decompressed images with increasing quantization step size. Figures 6-12 to 6-15 depict the experimental results (see also Appendix 7.1).

Figure 6-11: JPEG flower original image

Figure 6-12: JPEG flower image with global q-factor 1

SNR [dB]	22.92
R [%]	17.80
T_{comp} [s]	0.317
T_{decomp} [s]	0.317

Figure 6-13: JPEG flower image with global q-factor 6

SNR [dB]	17.25
R [%]	5.70
T_{comp} [s]	0.283
T_{decomp} [s]	0.267

Figure 6-14: JPEG flower image with global q-factor 12

SNR [dB]	15.22
R [%]	3.33
T_{comp} [s]	0.267
T_{decomp} [s]	0.250

Figure 6-15: JPEG flower image with global q-factor 20

SNR [dB]	14.18
R [%]	2.47
T_{comp} [s]	0.250
T_{decomp} [s]	0.250

The entire *flower* image contains a large amount of fine detail. There are no large homogeneous areas. Blossoms, leaves, and stalks of different shape and color characterize the image.

Again, a quantization factor of 1 does not cause any harm to the image reconstruction. The compression is already considerable, i.e., the image shrank to 17.80% of its original storage size. Beginning with quantization factor 6, visual distortions in the form of blocking artifacts cover more and more of the image. Since the image is highly complex, the quantization process destroys valuable image information spread over each DCT coefficient. The fairly coarse quantization tables, containing high values, are responsible for this degradation of visual quality. The different color shades are also affected by the quantization. Compare the *flower* image in Figure 6-13 and the *palace* image in Figure 6-7. The SNR for the *flower* image is 17.25 whereas the SNR for the *palace* image is 19.24, i.e., the decompressed image for *flower* is a little worse in quality.

The degree of compression compared to the palace image reflects the higher image complexity. It is always less for *flower*, e.g., R=17.80% versus 10.78% for quantization step size 1. The values come closer for higher step sizes. The compression reaches R=2.47% versus R=2.27% for step size 20.

Figure 6-16 depicts the change in compression rate and compression and decompression times caused by higher quantization factors.

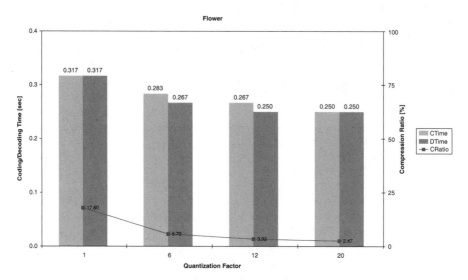

Figure 6-16: JPEG flower – summary of our results

6.4   Experiments with MPEG-1 Video Compression

Just as in JPEG we can use compression ratio R, compression time T_{comp} and decompression time T_{decomp} as quality measures for video compression algorithms. However, the visual distortion of motion now becomes a new quality criterion. As mentioned above, we will use a value Q_v to represent a combined, weighted measure for visual quality.

6.4.1 Computing the Visual Quality Measure Q_v

Ideally, a single measure should approximate the subjective quality perception of video sequences, as perceived by human beings. Definition of such a measure facilitates the automatic evaluation of the quality of a video transmission, or the output of a video codec. Once an objective measure is established, further video quality evaluations can be done without convening viewer panels and collecting subjective statistics.

Video applications, e.g., video-on-demand, could make use of the measure to establish different ratings of quality perceived by the viewer. At run-time, it might also serve as an indicator for digital transmission errors: randomly or periodically occurring noise would impair the visual quality, leading to reduced Q_v values. The storage-saving video compression process could be oriented towards minimum visual quality requirements: Parameters of the compression algorithm could be adjusted as soon as the measure falls short of a lower threshold. In our context we use Q_v to compare the output of various parameter sets for a given video codec, or, more generally, to compare different video compression techniques.

A visual quality measure for videos is a multi-dimensional operator. It must equally account for the impairment of the spatial and the temporal information. Loss in spatial information is indicated by blurry frames while jerky motion reveals loss in temporal information. But it is also possible to produce spurious information in compressed videos that did not exist in the original, e.g., false edges.

In [51] an objective video quality assessment system is described that emulates human perception. This is just one of several quality measures developed for video systems; many other are proposed in the literature (see for example [49]). For the measure described in [51] a test panel of viewers assessed and rated pairs of video sequences consisting of the original video streams and their degraded versions to determine the subjective quality perception. The categories were

(5) Imperceptible
(4) Perceptible but not annoying
(3) Slightly annoying
(2) Annoying
(1) Very annoying.

The results were then used to define quality parameters that correlated well with the viewing panel results. We define our quality measure Q_v, as in [51], as follows

$$Q_v = 4.77 - 0.992m_1 - 0.272m_2 - 0.356m_3,$$

where m_1, m_2 and m_3 are complementary measures that depict the amount of spatial and temporal information of a video scene.

Measure m_1 extracts the spatial information that is gained or lost in the frame in the course of the compression process. The underlying operator is the Sobel filter, an edge enhancement filter. Both the original and the degraded test series are filtered.

The spatial information feature, $SI[F_n]$, is given by

$$SI[F_n] = STD_{space}\{Sobel[F_n]\},$$

where STD_{space} is the standard deviation operator over the horizontal and vertical spatial dimensions in a frame, and F_n is the nth frame in the video sequence. The Sobel filter is defined by

$$Sobel_x = \begin{bmatrix} 1 & 2 & 1 \\ 0 & 0 & 0 \\ -1 & -2 & -1 \end{bmatrix}, \text{ and } Sobel_y = \begin{bmatrix} 1 & 0 & -1 \\ 2 & 0 & -2 \\ 1 & 0 & -1 \end{bmatrix},$$

where the Sobel filter for horizontal lines is $Sobel_x$ and for vertical lines $Sobel_y$.
The video quality metric m_1 is finally defined as

$$m_1 = RMS_{time}\left(5.81 \left| \frac{SI[O_n] - SI[D_n]}{SI[O_n]} \right| \right),$$

where O_n denotes the nth frame of the original video sequence, D_n is the nth frame of the degraded video sequence, $SI[.]$ represents the spatial information feature, RMS_{time} indicates the root mean square time-collapsing function.

Higher values for $SI[.]$ indicate more spatial detail, that is, the occurrence of a larger amount of edges in a frame. $SI[O_n]$ topping $SI[D_n]$ is an indicator for spatial blurring.

Measures m_2 and m_3 account for distortions in the *temporal dimension*. These metrics are based upon the motion difference image, ΔF_n, which is composed of the difference between pixel values at the same location in space but in consecutive frames. ΔF_n is given by

$$\Delta F_n = F_n - F_{n-1} .$$

The temporal information, $TI[F_n]$, is defined as the standard deviation of the motion difference image, and given by

$$TI[F_n] = STD_{space}[\Delta F_n].$$

The more motion is present between adjacent frames, the higher is the resulting $TI[F_n]$. Responsible for a loss in motion are, e.g., bandwidth constraints that force the codec to repeat parts of a frame. As soon as the complete frame information is updated the viewer perceives this fact as jerky motion. High quantization factors for a compressed video sequence can also contribute to loss in motion because the quantization equalizes pixel values within a frame. This is likely to lead to decreasing frame differences.

$$m_2 = f_{time}\left[0.108 * MAX\{(TI[O_n] - TI[D_n], 0)\}\right]$$

where

$$f_{time}(x_t) = STD_{time}\{CONV(x_t, [-1, 2, -1])\} ,$$

and $TI[F_n]$ is the temporal information operator, $CONV$ denotes the convolution operator, and STD_{time} depicts a standard deviation across time. m_2 only measures loss in motion energy, that is, added motion information is discarded. To enhance the change in motion a high pass filter (convolution operator) is applied.

Finally, m_3 is responsible for tracking down the largest added motion, e.g., random or periodic noise, or jerky motion introduced by digital transmission errors. m_3 is given by

$$m_3 = MAX_{\text{time}}\left\{ 4.23 * LOG_{10}\left(\frac{TI\lfloor D_n \rfloor}{TI\lfloor O_n \rfloor} \right) \right\},$$

where MAX_{time} returns the maximum value of the time history.

We supplemented the MPEG software codec used in our experiments by adding the computation of Q_v; this is much more efficient than computing Q_v by a separate tool because most of the relevant data is already available during the MPEG compression steps. The values computed by the modified MPEG codec were written to a file for later processing.

6.4.2 The MPEG-1 Codec

For our MPEG experiments we used the MPEG-1 software codec available from PVRG [40]. Like JPEG, each DCT coefficient has a separate quantization table entry (see Tables 6-3 and 6-4). These tables are applied to both the luminance and the chrominance components. In addition, there is again a global quantization factor. This spectral quantization is designed to reduce image quality distortion. As with our JPEG experiments, we have only modified the global factor; the quantization tables remained unchanged.

All software codecs developed by PVRG have the property that motion vector search ranges are specified as diameters and not as radiuses. Thus if we set the search range parameter to 8 we look for similar blocks in the neighborhood of ± 4 pixels.

Table 6-3: MPEG-1 quantization table for intra-coded macroblocks

8	16	19	22	26	27	29	34
16	16	22	24	27	29	34	37
19	22	26	27	29	34	34	38
22	22	26	27	29	34	37	40
22	26	27	29	32	35	40	48
26	27	29	32	35	40	48	58
26	27	29	34	38	46	56	69
27	29	35	38	46	56	69	83

Table 6-4: MPEG-1 quantization table for inter-coded macroblocks

16	16	16	16	16	16	16	16
16	16	16	16	16	16	16	16
16	16	16	16	16	16	16	16
16	16	16	16	16	16	16	16
16	16	16	16	16	16	16	16
16	16	16	16	16	16	16	16
16	16	16	16	16	16	16	16
16	16	16	16	16	16	16	16

We applied various parameter sets to the two video sequences *market* and *flower*. The *market* video contains object motion. People move across the scene. This motion occurs only locally; most of the scene is not affected. Fine-grain structures all over each frame characterize this video. In the following, we mainly use the *flower* video sequence to illustrate the impact of the various parameters, occasionally referring to the *market* video for comparison. The nature of the *flower* sequence using camera panning is a better example to examine motion compensation.

In the figures of this section, the following abbreviations for picture patterns are used:

Intra = IIII,   IP = IPPP,   IB = IBBB,   BP = IBBPBB.

The parameters of each series and the corresponding results are depicted in tables. In addition, results are illustrated with diagrams. For a complete overview on the experimental results, see Appendix 7-2.

When we planned our measurements we faced the problem of selecting and presenting interesting series of results from the multi-dimensional parameter space. As discussed in detail in Chapter 5, the MPEG and H.261 video compression algorithms have many adjustable parameters. If we take MPEG-1 as an example, we could modify

- ❑ the picture pattern (GOP structure),
- ❑ the quantization factor (global scaling factor),
- ❑ the motion vector search range.

We did so for each of our example videos. This led to a huge number of measurement results. In order to allow a better understanding of the effects of each parameter, we present separate series of measurement results where only one parameter changes in each series; all others are held constant.

6.4.3 Series 1: Influence of the Quantization Factor

In a first series of experiments, we show how visual quality, compression ratio, compression time and decompression time depend on the quantization factor. For the inter-coded video sequences, we keep the motion vector search range constant at 1. If the reader has access to the CD-ROM, the visual quality can be seen using an MPEG player. We also provide the Q_v values for each example, as discussed above.

Our experimental results for the *market* video clearly show that the quantization factor plays the key role in compressing the video stream. It significantly reduces the amount of data to be coded, leading to a high compression rate. Setting the quantization factor to a value of 1 already leads to a compression rate ranging from 53.85% (*market*: intra-coded) to 25.51% (*market*: IB pattern, see Appendix 7.2.1). Quantizing the DCT-coded sample values yields many zero values per 8 × 8 pixel block. In connection with zig-zag reordering and run-length encoding, the quantized DCT coefficients can be coded efficiently. At the highest quantization step size of 31, MPEG compression using intra-coding achieved a compression rate of 8.64% (*flower*). The best result was achieved with the BP picture pattern with a compression rate of 2.27% (*flower*).

The smaller amount of data to be coded also has a favorable effect on the compression and decompression time. The compression time was reduced by 5% to 15% when we changed the quantization factor from 1 to 31. Changing the quantization factor also made a tremendous difference in decompression time, which decreased between 45% and 57%, depending on the picture pattern. This is a consequence of the enormous decrease in the compression ratio, namely by 80% to 90%. The decompression times are far lower than the compression times, e.g., 66.2 s versus 342.0 s for intra-coding with quantization factor 1 (*market*). This confirms the asymmetric character of MPEG video coding.

Increasing the quantization factor leads to increasing artifacts within the video sequence, as the 8 × 8 pixel block becomes clearly recognizable. The blossoms appear blurry, whereas the lawn area is covered with blocking artifacts associated with a change in color (e.g., green to ochre). The reason for the visual difference is the more complex structure of the blossoms that forces more quantized DCT coefficients to be non-zero. The more homogeneous lawn yields many more zero-valued coefficients, hence, more visible block artifacts. The color dispersion occurs because the chrominance components go through the same compression process. Quantization with the quantization tables mentioned above still achieves acceptable compression results.

Motion-compensated videos are considerably more susceptible to blocking artifacts. In this case, the compression process is applied to the prediction error (original minus predicted values). Those values are more likely to be close to zero; the quantization actually sets most of them to zero.

Let us take a closer look at the number of zero and non-zero coefficients per 8 × 8 pixel block. Table 6-5 depicts the average number of non-zero coefficients per block. The MPEG codec provides the average values for an 8 × 8 pixel block by computing the average over all blocks of a frame. A block contains 64 coefficients. The results were computed for the intra-coding mode to preclude possible side effects from the motion compensation process. Pure intra-coding best reflects the video characteristics. When we analyzed the *flower* clip we determined three different sections in the clip that corresponded to the changing picture contents along the panning of the camera: the dominance in the scene is shifting from blossoms in the flowerbed to the surrounding lawn and back to the blossoms. The decreasing non-zero values illustrate the compression power of increasing quantization factors. Also, the table shows that the constant but heterogeneous *market* scene produces fairly constant bit rates per frame. Remember that object motion occurs only locally. In contrast, the camera panning of the *flower* video produces variable bit rates. Starting with the flowerbed in the center of the scene, the homogeneous lawn exposed to the sun (top of the picture) becomes increasingly dominant. During the panning, the more homogeneous lawn area more than compensates for the complex *flower* structures that dominated the picture at the beginning. This fact leads to a decreasing number of non-zero coefficients.

Figure 6-17 illustrates the change in the number of non-zero coefficients over time. For the *market* and the *flower* video, the non-zero numbers were computed for the three quantization factors 1, 15, and 31. The constant number of bits per block of the *market* scene (Ma) is clearly visible in the diagram. The change of complexity in the *flower* video (Fl) can also be observed in the figure. At first, the flowerbed with its complex structure is dominant. As panning progresses, the more homogeneous lawn comes into sight. From this point on, the *flower* video is more compressible than the market video.

Table 6-5: MPEG-1 – Average number of non-zero DCT coefficients per 8x8 block

	Q-factor 1	Q-factor 15	Q-factor 31
market	33	14	9
flower 1-50	34	14	9
flower 51-100	31	12	8
flower 101-150	30	12	7

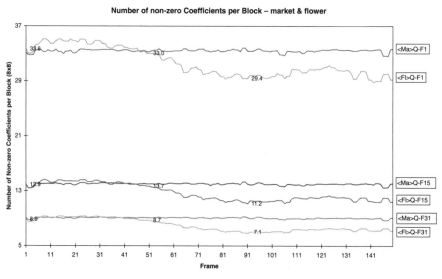

Figure 6-17: MPEG Intra – number of non-zero coefficients

As mentioned before, the measurement results for each series are presented in the form of a table and a graph. The quality and performance measures Q_v, R, T_{comp} and T_{decomp} are those defined above.

In a first step we analyze the effects of a variable quantization factor on compression rate and compression and decompression times for the intra-coded *flower* scene; parameters and results are depicted in Table 6-6 and Figure 6-18. Figure 6-18 shows a decrease of the size of a compressed image from 48.71% to 8.64% of the original image with increasing quantization factor. Since all frames are intra-coded the quantization factor plays a dominant role for the achievable compression ratio. The graph also shows very clearly the asymmetric behavior of the MPEG intra-coding algorithm: compression times are always much higher than decompression times. When we increase the quantization factors the compression times decrease slightly because coefficients are increasingly set to zero. Thus, the Huffman-based run-length coding is simplified and can take advantage of long runs of zero-valued coefficients.

Table 6-6: MPEG-1 Series 1 flower – results for picture pattern Intra

Picture pattern	IIII		
Q-factor	1	15	31
Q_v	4.764	4.757	4.726
R [%]	48.71	14.92	8.64
T_{comp} [s]	420.5	403.8	398.1
T_{decomp} [s]	62.8	39.4	34.6

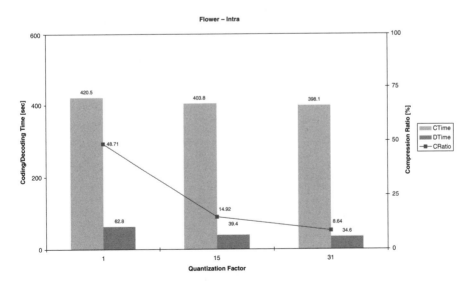

Figure 6-18: MPEG-1 Series 1 flower – results for Intra

Next, we look at the IP picture pattern (see Table 6-7 and Figure 6-19). We now apply inter-coding with a motion vector search range set to 1, the lower bound required by our MPEG codec. By using a motion vector of 1 we already gain significantly lower compression rates compared to intra-coding, as indicated in Figure 6-19. For example, we now obtain a compression ratio of 34.34% instead of 48.71% for the intra-coding mode (see Figure 6-18). The slow, steady camera panning introduces only limited changes on a macroblock basis between two consecutive frames. Consequently, the motion compensation process can efficiently compress a macroblock based on the prediction error. The improvements using the IP picture pattern are also reflected by the compression and decompression times, e.g., $T_{comp} = 337.2$ s and $T_{decomp} = 51.7$ s for q-factor 1 as opposed to $T_{comp} = 420.5$ s and $T_{decomp} = 62.8$ s for the intra mode. The minimum value of 1 for the motion vector search range imposes no burden on the motion estimation unit of our MPEG codec. The macroblock comparisons required by the motion compensation process could be performed quickly. This fact, combined with the smaller amount of data to be coded using the prediction error, led to the far better results when compared with the Intra picture pattern.

Table 6-7: MPEG-1 Series 1 flower – results for picture pattern IP

Picture pattern	IPPP		
Motion vector search range	1		
Q-factor	1	15	31
Q_v	4.764	4.741	4.707
R [%]	34.34	8.67	4.67
T_{comp} [s]	337.2	309.3	299.3
T_{decomp} [s]	51.7	30.1	25.4

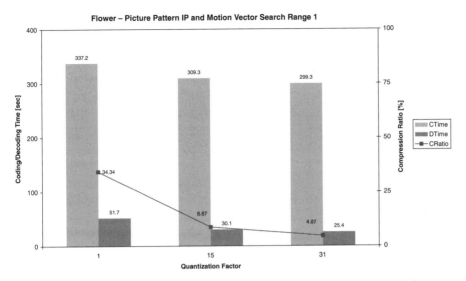

Figure 6-19: MPEG-1 Series 1 flowers – results for picture pattern IP and motion vector search range 1

Inter-coding using the bi-directional interpolation option is the next subject of evaluation (see Table 6-8 and Figure 6-20). Defining B-pictures in the group of pictures enables the codec to choose either forward prediction or backward prediction or bi-directional interpolation as coding mode for a macroblock (16×16 pixels, or four 8×8 pixel blocks of the luminance component). Or, if none of those inter-coding modes can provide satisfactory results, normal intra-coding is applied to the macroblock. This decision process takes time, as we can clearly read from Figure 6-20. The compression times were significantly worse compared to the IP picture pattern. For example, for quantization step size 1 we obtained $T_{comp} = 476.0$ s (IB) versus $T_{comp} = 337.2$ s (IP). But with respect to the compression ratio R the IB picture pattern clearly outperforms the IP mode, ranging from $R = 27.4\%$ to $R = 3.30\%$ (IB) versus $R = 34.34\%$ to $R = 4.67\%$ (IP). The decompression times are comparable. As a conclusion, it is advantageous to define B-frames in the group of pictures to receive lower compression ratios.

Table 6-8: MPEG-1 Series 1 flower – results for picture pattern IB

Picture pattern	IBBB		
Motion vector search range	1		
Q-factor	1	15	31
Q_v	4.752	4.710	4.675
R [%]	27.40	5.88	3.30
T_{comp} [s]	476.0	445.9	438.9
T_{decomp} [s]	48.2	27.7	24.4

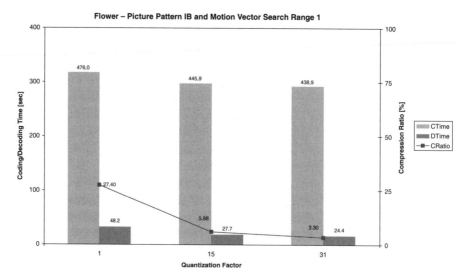

Figure 6-20: MPEG-1 Series 1 flower – results for picture pattern IB and motion vector search range 1

We can derive from the results for the IB picture pattern above the fact that the use of B-frames improves the compression ratio significantly. The drawback is the amount of time that is necessary for the compression process.

We now investigate a picture pattern that combines P- and B-frames (see Table 6-9 and Figure 6-21). The compression ratios of the BP picture pattern are comparable to the IB picture pattern, and superior to the IP picture pattern. While the exclusive use of B-frames is better for quantization factor 1 ($R = 27.40\%$ for IB versus $R = 30.80\%$ for IP), the quantization factors 15 and 31 deliver contrary results with the BP picture pattern slightly better than IB ($R = 5.82\%$ and $R = 3.06\%$ versus $R = 5.88\%$ and $R = 3.30\%$). With higher quantization factors that cause almost all of the coefficients of the prediction error to be set to zero, the more frequently occurring reference I-frames and the overhead for interpolated macroblocks (with its associated two motion vectors) make the BP picture pattern slightly better than the IB mode. But if we look at the compression times the BP picture pattern achieved significantly better results, e.g., $T_{comp} = 434.9$ s versus $T_{comp} = 476.0$ s for q-factor 1. Associated with the almost identical compression ratios, the decompression times differed only slightly.

Table 6-9: MPEG-1 Series 1 flower – results for picture pattern BP

Picture pattern	IBBPBB		
Motion vector search range	1		
Q-factor	1	15	31
Q_v	4.758	4.713	4.668
R [%]	30.80	5.82	3.06
T_{comp} [s]	434.9	400.3	387.4
T_{decomp} [s]	51.9	28.7	23.8

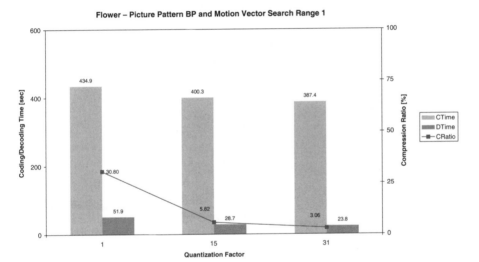

Figure 6-21: MPEG-1 Series 1 flower – results for picture pattern BP and motion vector search range 1

6.4.4 Series 2: Influence of the Motion Vector Search Range

In the next series of experiments we show how visual quality, compression ratio, compression time, and decompression time are affected by the choice of the motion vector search range. We keep the quantization factor constant at 15. If the reader has access to the CD-ROM, the visual quality can be seen using an MPEG player. We also provide the Q_v values for each example in the result table.

Tables 6-10 to 6-12 and Figures 6-22 to 6-24 show several interesting details. The compression time increased significantly when we increased the motion vector search range. For example, the coding of the clip with the BP picture pattern takes T_{comp} = 400.3 s for the motion vector search of 1 versus

T_{comp} = 527.4 s for the motion vector search range of 8. This is quite plausible, because the time to perform the search for a matching block increases with the search range. If no best-match can be found within the range, simple intra-coding is applied to the macroblock. The panning across our flowerbed is a perfect example for a sequence of frames where matches can often be found in the 8-pixel neighborhood.

Whereas the compression rate for the IP picture pattern is nearly constant (R = 8.09% to 8.67%), the results for IB and BP differ more significantly for the three search ranges (R = 5.00% to 5.88% and R = 4.48% to 5.82%). The forward prediction of IP has difficulties detecting the motion in the motion-intensive *flower* video. The additional possibility of backward prediction and interpolation enhances the chance of finding a good match (small prediction error). Yet, the macroblocks are coded very much the same, no matter which motion vector direction is used. Examining the statistics provided by the codec explains this characteristic. Often, either motion compensation with motion vector 0 (inter-coding is applied but no motion compensation takes place, also called *inter-frame compensation*) was used, because it already complied with the threshold for compensation or intra-coding was finally applied after all other options failed to result in acceptable prediction errors.

The decompression times reflect the compression rate results. This fact is quite obvious, since decompression time depends on the previously achieved compression rate: the more data we have to decompress, the slower it typically goes.

Due to the characteristics just mentioned the visual quality Q_v also does not vary much for the three motion vectors within each picture pattern series.

Let us now start our analysis with picture pattern IP (see Table 6-10 and Figure 6-22). Figure 6-22 illustrates that the impact of the motion vector search range on the compression ratio is only marginal; the absolute change of R is only 0.58%. The explanation is that the prediction error is mostly already below a given threshold when no motion vector is used, i.e., a macroblock is inter-coded without motion compensation (*inter-frame compensation*). The statistics provided by the MPEG codec indicated that this option of encoding a macroblock was frequently used. Thus, lower prediction errors that could be found with increasing search ranges are not of further interest. Yet, sometimes the codec had to check for quite some time to get a prediction error below this given threshold. We also observed during our experiments that no acceptable match (prediction error below threshold) was found; therefore that macroblock was intra-coded. This accounted for the huge differences in compression times, e.g., T_{comp} = 309.3 s versus T_{comp} = 352.9 s versus T_{comp} = 381.7 s as depicted in Figure 6-22.

Table 6-10: MPEG-1 Series 2 flower – results for picture pattern IP and q-factor 15

Picture pattern	IPPP		
Quantization factor	15		
Motion vector	1	8	15
Q_v	4.741	4.739	4.738
R [%]	8.67	8.17	8.09
T_{comp} [s]	309.3	352.9	381.7
T_{decomp} [s]	30.1	29.6	29.5

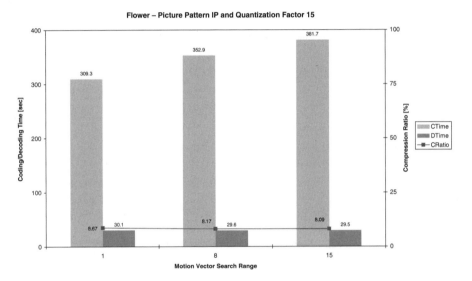

Figure 6-22: MPEG-1 Series 2 flower – results for picture pattern IP and q-factor 15

As in the previous section, we continue our series with the picture pattern IB using bidirectional interpolation (see Table 6-11 and Figure 6-23). As we increased the motion vector search range, we observed a significant increase in compression time. This was true for each of the picture patterns we used. We obtained the highest increase for picture pattern IB (see Figure 6-23). This is quite plausible because the search area must be checked using forward prediction, backward prediction, and bi-directional interpolation. All this adds up to long compression times.

Table 6-11: MPEG-1 Series 2 flower – results for picture pattern IB and q-factor 15

Picture pattern	IBBB		
Quantization factor	15		
Motion vector	1	8	15
Q_v	4.710	4.703	4.703
R [%]	5.88	5.18	5.00
T_{comp} [s]	445.9	624.4	781.8
T_{decomp} [s]	27.7	26.6	26.2

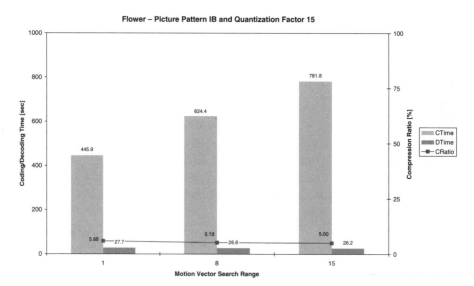

Figure 6-23: MPEG-1 Series 2 flower – results for picture pattern IB and q-factor 15

We conclude this series with the remaining BP picture pattern using parameters as depicted in Table 6-12.

Figure 6-24 shows that the compression ratios are comparable to the IB picture pattern, e.g., R = 5.82% (BP) versus R = 5.88% (IB) using a motion vector of 1. The results for the compression times were between the results for the IP and the IB picture pattern but more similar to IB. This was always true for each of our compression time results. This fact was caused by the time-consuming computations for each of the motion compensation options.

Table 6-12: MPEG-1 Series 2 – flower – results for picture pattern BP and q-factor 15

Picture pattern	IBBPBB		
Quantization factor	15		
Motion vector	1	8	15
Q_v	4.713	4.708	4.707
R [%]	5.82	4.79	4.48
T_{comp} [s]	400.3	527.4	641.2
T_{decomp} [s]	28.7	26.8	26.4

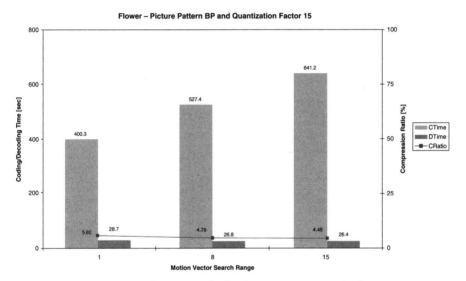

Figure 6-24: MPEG-1 Series 2 flower – results for picture pattern BP and q-factor 15

6.4.5 Series 3: Influence of the Picture Pattern

In the last series of experiments, we illustrate how visual quality, compression ratio, compression time, and decompression time are influenced by the MPEG picture pattern. We keep both the motion vector (8) and the quantization factor (15) at constant values. If the reader has access to the CD-ROM, the visual quality can be seen using an MPEG player. We also provide the Q_v values for each experiment.

The comparison of the picture patterns shows the expected results (see Table 6-13 and Figure 6-25). The IP picture pattern (IPPP) solely applies predictive motion compensation (using a reference frame in the past to predict the future). The IB picture pattern (IBBB) applies bidirectional motion compensation (a reference frame in the past and/or in the future). The BP picture pattern (IBBPBB) provides a predicted frame between two intra-frames as a reference frame.

    The best compression time was achieved with the IP picture pattern (solely predictive). The IB was the worst picture pattern because of the many B-frames: those require a very complex and time-consuming computation process. On the other hand, the chances improve to get a good match, hence, a small prediction error. Therefore, the IB and BP picture pattern topped the IP picture pattern with respect to decompression time T_{decomp} and compression rate R. The reason for the almost identical results for the IB and BP picture pattern with respect to compression rate R, compression time T_{comp} and decompression time T_{decomp} were already elaborated in Section 6.4.4. The BP picture pattern was always comparable to the IB picture pattern with respect to the compression rates achieved, and with respect to the compression times its results were between the picture patterns IP and IB but closer to IB. As an example, those facts are illustrated in Figure 6-25.

Table 6-13: MPEG-1 Series 3 flower – results for motion vector 8 and q-factor 15

Motion vector search range	8		
Quantization factor	15		
Picture pattern	**IP**	**IB**	**BP**
Q_v	4.739	4.703	4.708
$R\,[\%]$	8.17	5.18	4.79
$T_{comp}\,[s]$	352.9	624.4	527.4
$T_{decomp}\,[s]$	29.6	26.6	26.8

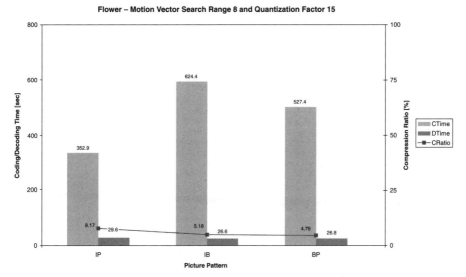

Figure 6-25: MPEG-1 Series 3 flower – results for motion vector search range 8 and q-factor 15

6.4.6 Where do MPEG Codecs Spend Their Time?

It is interesting to analyze where a MPEG codec spends most of its encoding/decoding time; this processing step can then be optimized by manual code hacking, writing pieces of the code in assembler, or by providing special hardware. For example, an MPEG chip typically has special instructions to carry out the most critical pieces of the algorithms efficiently, and this makes MPEG video boards much more efficient than traditional CPUs when executing MPEG code. Many CPU manufacturers are currently planning to include special machine instructions in the next generation of their general-purpose RISC processors for efficient execution of MPEG code; these instructions will allow the machine to decode, or perhaps even encode, MPEG-2 in software in real-time.

To further investigate the influence of the parameters *global quantization factor* and *motion vector search range* on T_{comp} and T_{decomp}, we have compiled Figures 6-26 and 6-27, depicting the compression and decompression times and compression rate for q-factors of 1, 15, and 31 and for motion vector search ranges of 1, 8, and 15 pixels. The inter-coding mode with picture pattern IBBPBB is used in both figures.

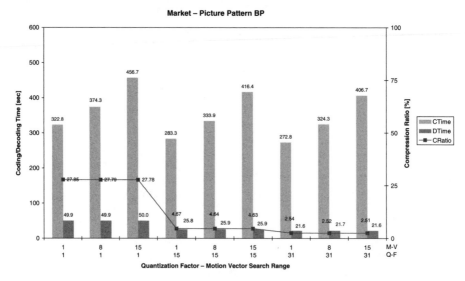

Figure 6-26: MPEG-1 market – results for picture pattern BP

Figure 6-26 was computed from the *market* video with object motion: people are moving between the market booths. It is surprising that motion vectors are obviously *not* used in the compression of this clip; the compression ratio is independent of the motion vector search ranges. We analyzed this example in detail and found that motion vectors were indeed computed by the codec. However, the subsequent comparison of the frames encoded with motion vectors showed a deviation from the original above the built-in quality threshold; thus the codec decided to discard the motion vectors and use intra-coding for all macroblocks instead. So we verified our assumption.

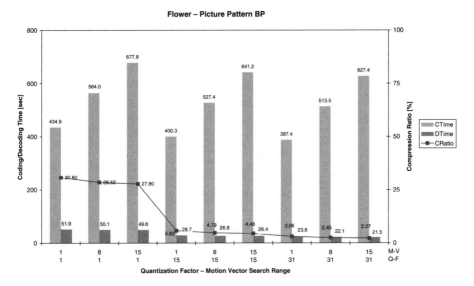

Figure 6-27: MPEG-1 flower – results for picture pattern BP

Figure 6-27 shows the results for the *flower* video, which contained camera motion (panning). In this case, there is so much lateral displacement of identical macroblocks that motion compensation works well. For example, with the global quantization factor set to 1, the compression ratio was improved from $R = 30.80\%$ to $R = 28.52\%$ to $R = 27.80\%$ when the search range was increased from 1 to 8, and 15, respectively. However, the increase of encoding times from $T_{comp} = 434.9$ s to $T_{comp} = 677.8$ s for the scene of 150 frames shows how expensive motion estimation really is on the encoding side. We conclude that large motion vector search ranges can only be applied where the *encoding delay* is not critical: examples include compression for CD-ROMs and video-on-demand servers, but not for videoconferencing.

6.5 Experiments with H.261 Video Compression

The H.261 experiments were conducted in the same manner as for MPEG-1. Examples for the visual quality are not be shown on the CD-ROM accompanying this book because we cannot expect our readers to have an H.261 player. As in the case of MPEG-1, we mostly use the *flower* clip (see Figure 6-4) to illustrate our results. As explained in Chapter 5, the H.261 standard does not allow to select a picture pattern for inter-frame coding; it employs forward prediction on a frame-by-frame basis only. To prevent infinite error propagation, a macroblock must be intra-coded at least once in every 132 transmitted frames (forced updating). We again present measurement series where we vary the parameters *quantization factor* and *motion vector search range.* Unlike MPEG-1, H.261 only employs a global quantization factor (scaling factor); spectral quantization with a matrix of quantization factors is not specified in the standard. In the following, the intra-frame and the inter-frame coding modes are referred to as *Intra* and *Inter.*

The parameters of each series and the corresponding results are again depicted in tables and diagrams. Remember that motion vector search ranges are specified as diameters and not as radiuses, as explained above.

6.5.1   Series 1: Influence of the Quantization Factor

In a first series of experiments we show how compression ratio R, compression time T_{comp} and decompression time T_{decomp} depend on the quantization factor. We keep the motion vector search range at 1 for the inter-coding mode.

As expected, the image quality deteriorates with increasing quantization factors. It heavily influences the motion-compensated macroblocks with even worse visual quality. The identical treatment of all DCT coefficients, applying one global quantization factor to all of them, causes clearly visible blocking artifacts.

Tables 6-15 and 6-16 and Figures 6-28 and 6-29 demonstrate diverging compression time results. On the one hand, Intra leads to slightly increasing compression times (T_{comp} = 416.1 s to 417.6 s). On the other hand, for Inter, increasing quantization factors yield a significantly shorter compression time (T_{comp} = 267.6 s versus T_{comp} = 222.5 s). Global quantization cannot achieve advantageous output for the subsequent entropy encoding step. Similar results were obtained for the *market* video.

Increasing quantization factors cause significantly better compression ratios ranging from R = 66.37% to R = 3.65% for Intra and from R = 48.78% to R = 2.33% for Inter. The decompression times again reflect the respective compression ratios.

Analysis of the quantization factor is also complemented by a closer look at the number of zero and non-zero coefficients per 8×8 pixel block. Table 6-14 depicts the average number of non-zero coefficients per block. The H.261 codec provides the mean values for an 8×8 pixel block by computing the average over all blocks of a frame. The values are shown for the intra-frame coding mode. When we processed the *flower* clip we decomposed it into three different sections that corresponded to changing picture contents: the view shifting from blossoms of the flowerbed to the surrounding lawn and back to blossoms. The decreasing non-zero values illustrate the compression power of increasing quantization factors: coarse quantization leads to long runs of zeroes in the zig-zag traversal of the matrix of coefficients. These long runs are compressed very well by the subsequent run-length/Huffman coding step.

Table 6-14 also shows that the steady but heterogeneous *market* scene produces fairly constant bit rates per frame. On the other hand, the camera panning of the *flower* video produces different bit rates. Starting with the flowerbed in the center of the scene, the *homogeneous* lawn exposed to the sun (top of the picture) becomes increasingly dominant. During the panning, the lawn more than compensates for the complex *flower* structures. Thus, the number of non-zero coefficients decreases.

The degree of compression achievable with quantization factor 31 outperforms the MPEG codec (compare Section 6.4.3). The findings for the two video sequences *market* and *flower* show almost identical results. Just two to three coefficients remained non-zero, the other 61 to 63 coefficients were quantized to zero.

Table 6-14: H.261 – Average number of non-zero coefficients per block

	Q-factor 1	Q-factor 15	Q-factor 31
Market	32	7	3
Flower 1-50	33	7	3
Flower 51-100	30	5	2
Flower 101-150	29	5	2

We now investigate the Intra coding mode for H.261. When we changed the quantization factor we obtained the results depicted in Table 6-15 and Figure 6-28. Figure 6-28 illustrates the tremendous impact of increasing the quantization step size; the compression ratio R decreases from 66.37% to only 3.65%. We also observe that the compression time is largely indifferent to the quantization factor: when we change the step size from 1 to 15 to 31 the compression times T_{comp} are 416.1 s, 409.0 s, and 417.6 s.

Table 6-15: H.261 Series 1 flower – results for coding mode Intra

Coding mode	Intra		
Q-factor	1	15	31
Q_v	4.758	4.717	4.559
R [%]	66.37	7.43	3.65
T_{comp} [s]	416.1	409.0	417.6
T_{decomp} [s]	57.0	22.6	20.3

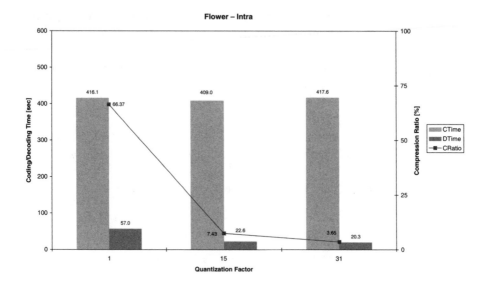

Figure 6-28: H.261 Series 1 flower – results for coding mode Intra

The compression ratios achieved by the intra-coded clips can be further improved when motion compensation is used. As already explained, the motion compensation unit tries to encode a macroblock by looking for another macroblock in the previous frame that matches it closely. In the case that such a matching macroblock is found, only the difference between the two macroblocks is coded (*prediction error*) together with the displacement information (*motion vector*). Table 6-16 and Figure 6-29 show the details for a motion vector search range of 1. The changes in the compression ratio were significant. For example, compared to intra-coding the compression ratio R decreased from 66.37% to 48.78% when step size 1 was applied. Another interesting observation can be made when looking at the compression times. In contrast to intra-coding, the compression times decreased when we increased the quantization factors; for step sizes 1, 15, and 31 we obtained for T_{comp} 267.6 s, 226.8 s, and 222.5 s.

A decrease of the compression time for the motion vector search range of 1 was also seen for the *market* clip. The improvements of the compression ratios changing from intra- to inter-coding also applied to the decompression times. No matter what quantization factor we used in our experiments, the decompression of inter-coded clips was always faster than the decompression of intra-coded clips. The gap is larger for the *market* clips, since they achieved lower compression ratios than the *flower* clips (see also Appendix 7-3). Less motion in the market scene was the cause of that property.

Table 6-16: H.261 Series 1 flower – results for coding mode Inter and motion vector search range 1

Coding mode	Inter		
Motion vector search range	1		
Q-factor	1	15	31
Q_v	4.759	4.715	4.557
R [%]	48.78	4.94	2.33
T_{comp} [s]	267.6	226.8	222.5
T_{decomp} [s]	47.8	18.3	16.2

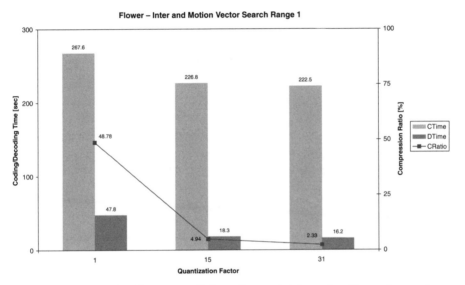

Figure 6-29: H.261 Series 1 flower – results for coding mode Inter and motion vector search range 1

6.5.2 Series 2: Influence of the Motion Vector Sector Search Range

Finally, we show the influence of the motion vector search range on compression ratio, compression time and decompression time for H.261 (see Table 6-17 and Figure 6-30). We keep the quantization factor value at 15.

For the *flower* video, increasing the motion vector search range has a major effect on the compression time. It peaks at T_{comp} = 389.9 s for quantization factor 31 starting with T_{comp} = 226.8 s for quantization step size 1. The increase in time also paid off with improving compression ratios, R = 3.72% instead of

$R = 4.94\%$. That improvement in compression ratio was largely due to the motion-intensive camera panning.

Object motion such as in the *market* video is much harder to track down for the motion estimation unit. As a result, we achieved constant compression ratios for *market* for increasing motion vector search ranges (see also Appendix 7.3). As usual, the decompression times remained constant; of course, the reproduction of a (predicted) macroblock elsewhere in the image costs the same amount of time no matter how far away from the earlier position the macroblock is. In other words, the length of motion vectors has no influence on decompression time.

We observed an interesting characteristic when we compared the compression times of all intra- and inter-coded clips: the compression times of inter-coded clips were always superior to the intra-coded clips (see also Appendix 7.3). The savings in the amount of data to be transmitted after compression compensated the time required for the motion compensation, no matter what motion vector search range we used. This result is in contrast to the MPEG-1 findings when picture pattern IBBB and IBBPBB were used (see also Appendix 7.2). The explanation for the superiority of H.261 in this case is that it does not define *backward prediction* or *interpolation*; consequently, no future reference frames are necessary. Here, motion compensation is performed as *forward prediction* on a frame-by-frame basis. Therefore, the codec does not have to wait for a future reference frame before it can continue the compression process. When we employed the IPPP picture pattern for our MPEG-1 experiments the results were similar to H.261 because the mechanisms were the same.

Table 6-17: H.261 Series 2 flower – results for coding mode Inter and q-factor 15

Coding mode	Inter		
Quantization factor	15		
Motion vector search range	1	15	31
Q_v	4.715	4.718	4.702
R [%]	4.94	4.89	3.72
T_{comp} [s]	226.8	277.7	389.9
T_{decomp} [s]	18.3	19.2	20.3

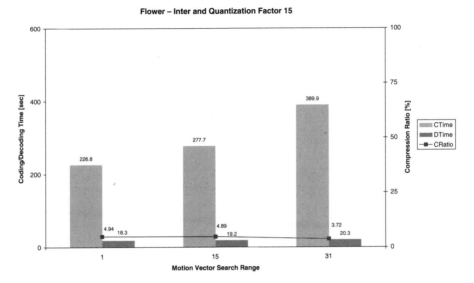

Figure 6-30: H.261 Series 2 flower – results for coding mode Inter and q-factor 15

6.6 Video Quality Measurement Results

The reader has probably noticed that we have not discussed the objective video quality measure Q_v so far. The reason is that the results of Q_v did not lead to a reasonable distinction of visual quality. We obtained very similar results for the various series of experiments, no matter what parameters we used.

We expected to get better results (i.e., better values of Q_v) for the *flower* video because of our own viewing assessments. Although the *flower* video depicts a panning across a flowerbed, its smooth nature does not cause the video codec to output jerky motion. Our emphasis was on video compression rather than video transmission, so we did not restrict the bandwidth. The *market* video, on the other hand, contains many more edge changes, a parameter that should influence Q_v. Also, local motion in the form of moving people characterizes the video scenes.

In general, we expected higher quantization factors to result in lower values for Q_v since more spatial detail gets lost.

The Q_v results for the *flower* and *market* video are compared in Figure 6-31. With respect to the relative values for the two clips, we see our expectations confirmed: The *flower* video has a better quality than the *market* video. Lower values for Q_v are the result of higher quantization factors. A change in the motion vector search range influences the outcome for Q_v just as little as the compression ratio did (see Section 6.4).

Surprising are the absolute values of Q_v. They always indicate an excellent visual quality regarding the classification from (1) to (5) proposed by the developers of the measure. It is assumed that the results are rounded before they get assigned to one of the categories. So, each set of compression parameters for both video sequences would yield quality level *imperceptible* (5). But both video scenes are visually distorted by the compression process. The *flower* video shows few but visible distortions if watched carefully from a short distance. Blocking artifacts appear more clearly in the *market* video in the area of the people in motion.

Loss in spatial and temporal information in the form of a decreasing number of edges within the frames and less motion energy as a result of the video compression are indicated by the quality metrics m_1 and m_2 for both video scenes. In addition, m_3 proves the clearly visible existence of jerky motion in the *market* video. m_3 can be neglected for the *flower* video which truly reflects the visual impression. The motion in the video scenes occurs either locally and jerkily (*market*), or globally and smoothly (*flower*). The influence on the objective quality measure Q_v should therefore be limited even if local motion (*market*) does not appear to receive its fair share (due to the standard deviation calculated over the entire frame). Spatial information impairments are not well reflected either. The problem appears to be the high number of edges in the original as well as in the degraded version, especially in the *market* video. Thus, the highly weighted metric m_1 (0.992) is only of marginal importance in our context.

More specifically, the marginal change in edge occurrence in compressed frames is caused by the compression characteristics of MPEG-1. Like H.261 and JPEG, MPEG-1 produces blocking artifacts with increasing quantization factors. This simply means that edges are created. Therefore, the *Sobel* filter cannot provide meaningful information with respect to the visual video quality. In other words, the creation of blocks with sharp edges is judged as an indicator of good quality by Q_v. The result is supported by tests with JPEG-encoded video sequences where the output consisted completely of distorted frames (mostly monochrome 8×8 pixel blocks). Spatial detail was completely discarded. The spatial information feature in Q_v showed hardly any difference, with a relative decrease of 4%.

It is mentioned in [51] that further research is intended. One extension should be the emphasis of local image subregions for the extraction of spatial and temporal information. These subregions can be horizontal or vertical stripes, a rectangular region, or the like. In our opinion, and based on our test results, the video quality metrics should also be adapted to codecs whose compression characteristics are block artifacts.

On the other hand, Q_v should very well characterize the quality results of wavelet-based compression, since its output becomes more and more blurry. Tests of the wavelet-based compression technique with Q_v are beyond the scope of this book.

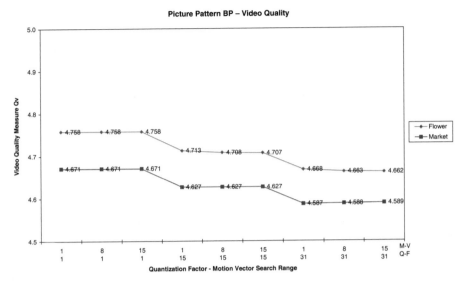

Figure 6-31: MPEG – results of the video quality measure Q$_v$ for picture pattern BP

6.7 Conclusions and Recommendations

In this chapter, we have discussed the impact of various parameter settings on visual quality, compression ratio, and compression and decompression time. The JPEG, MPEG-1, and H.261 codecs available to us belonged to the Public Video Research Group in Stanford, California. JPEG, MPEG-1, and H.261 are asymmetric compression standards. The decompression times are typically below the compression times, depending mostly on the previously achieved compression ratio. Deteriorating visual quality becomes visible in the form of blocking artifacts due to quantization.

Quantization plays a key role in the compression process. A careful combination of a global quantization factor and spectral quantization using quantization tables can achieve both acceptable visual quality and high compression ratios. H.261 only applies a global quantization factor (i.e., the same factor for all coefficients), leading to visually disturbing artifacts. Even though JPEG makes use of both quantization elements, the visual quality becomes fairly bad very soon because of the very high values of the quantization table entries compared to MPEG-1 (those values were preset by the implementers of the codec). The visual quality of the compressed MPEG-1 videos is acceptable even for the highest quantization step size and B-frames. Of course, the choice of the picture pattern is very important here. Defining frequent I-frames as reference frames between P- and/or B-frames prevents error propagation in the form of blurry pictures and blocking artifacts.

In our discussion of the JPEG findings, we put the focus on the analysis of compression effects on images with and without sharp edges. The compressed versions of the *palace* image clearly showed the loss in edge sharpness. The homogeneous areas of the image could be reconstructed well, with only small distortions in color. On the other hand, the complex *flower* image structure with no larger homogeneous areas was unrecognizable at the highest quantization step size; too many of the block coefficients bearing important information for reconstructing the image were discarded.

Examining the MPEG-1 picture patterns, we demonstrated the vast impact of B-frames on compression time. Combining B- and P-frames (IBBPBB) produced results in between the picture patterns IBBB and IPPP.

Increasing the motion vector search range can only achieve further compression in case of camera motion (*flower* video). Object motion, stochastic in nature, is too hard to detect for the motion estimation unit (*market* video). For object motion, the macroblocks are often intra-coded (as in I-frames). This led to constant compression ratios using different motion vector search ranges for the *market* video. That interesting result could be observed for MPEG-1 and H.261 alike. The compression times react extremely sensitively to a change in the motion vector search range.

With respect to compression ratio, the inter-frame coding mode of H.261 was superior to the inter-frame coding of MPEG-1. Remember that the H.261 standard stipulates the intra-coding of a particular macroblock once in every 132 transmitted frames (MPEG-1 adopted this technique). As well as the different coding mode strategies, the coarse-grain quantization of H.261 helps to achieve much better compression results. The consequence is significantly worse visual quality. The H.261 codec also outperformed the MPEG codec with respect to the compression times achieved when motion compensation was applied. The motion compensation of H.261 is done on a frame-by-frame basis, i.e., for adjacent frames only. For intra-coding, the results were similar.

As an overall conclusion, we could say: If the emphasis is on well-preserved visual quality, MPEG-1 is the best choice. Shifting the focus towards high compression ratios and minimum compression times, H.261 is preferable.

This concludes the presentation and discussion of our measurement results. It is interesting to note that the compression algorithms are discussed in many textbooks in great detail, but very little is published about the *optimization strategy* implemented in the encoders. Whereas the decoding process is largely determined by the incoming data stream, the *encoder* has many options to choose from, all in conformance with the standard. It seems that the optimal selection of encoding parameters, as a function of the application scenario, is not yet well understood. More research is needed here. Perhaps our experimental results can at least give some hints toward that goal.

7 Appendix

7.1 Table of JPEG Measurement Results

	QF	CodTime [s]	DecTime [s]	SNR	Size [bytes]	CR [%]
Palace	1	0.283	0.283	21.07	16,392	10.78
	6	0.267	0.267	19.24	6,138	4.04
	12	0.267	0.233	17.68	4,191	2.76
	20	0.250	0.233	16.73	3,447	2.27
Flower	1	0.317	0.317	22.92	27,060	17.80
	6	0.283	0.267	17.25	8,666	5.70
	12	0.267	0.250	15.22	5,066	3.33
	20	0.250	0.250	14.18	3,757	2.47

QF = Quantization Factor
CodTime/DecTime = Coding/Decoding Time [sec]
CR = Compression Ratio (compressed/original*100) [%]
SNR = Signal-to-Noise Ratio

7.2 Table of MPEG-1 Measurement Results

7.2.1 Market Results

	QF	CodTime [s]	DecTime [s]	OVQ	Size [bytes]	CR [%]
Market	1	342.0	66.2	4.722	12,282,535	53.85
Intra	15	323.4	41.2	4.674	4,029,192	17.66
	31	317.9	36.0	4.661	2,422,894	10.62

	QF	MV	CodTime [s]	DecTime [s]	OVQ	Size [bytes]	CR [%]
Market	1	1	291.2	49.9	4.673	7,304,063	32.02
Inter	1	8	313.0	50.2	4.673	7,294,264	31.98
IP	1	15	348.6	50.3	4.673	7,291,858	31.97
	15	1	261.4	28.7	4.604	1,583,349	6.94
	15	8	284.4	28.5	4.605	1,574,591	6.90
	15	15	319.6	28.3	4.605	1,572,482	6.89
	31	1	247.4	22.3	4.551	818,092	3.59
	31	8	269.6	22.6	4.553	811,483	3.56
	31	15	310.7	22.5	4.553	809,829	3.55

	QF	MV	CodTime [s]	DecTime [s]	OVQ	Size [bytes]	CR [%]
Market	1	1	317.4	47.3	4.662	5,819,600	25.51
Inter	1	8	371.5	46.9	4.662	5,809,350	25.47
IB	1	15	459.0	47.0	4.662	5,807,850	25.46
	15	1	279.9	25.5	4.652	1,220,609	5.35
	15	8	334.3	25.5	4.653	1,215,360	5.33
	15	15	422.3	25.5	4.653	1,214,548	5.32
	31	1	274.4	22.7	4.613	723,188	3.17
	31	8	328.9	22.6	4.615	720,276	3.16
	31	15	416.9	22.8	4.615	719,901	3.16

	QF	MV	CodTime [s]	DecTime [s]	OVQ	Size [bytes]	CR [%]
Market	1	1	322.8	49.9	4.671	6,352,504	27.85
Inter	1	8	374.3	49.9	4.671	6,337,680	27.79
BP	1	15	456.7	50.0	4.671	6,336,294	27.78
	15	1	283.3	25.8	4.627	1,066,264	4.67
	15	8	333.9	25.9	4.627	1,057,621	4.64
	15	15	416.4	25.9	4.627	1,056,800	4.63
	31	1	272.8	21.6	4.587	579,543	2.54
	31	8	324.3	21.7	4.588	574,230	2.52
	31	15	406.7	21.6	4.589	573,612	2.51

QF	= Quantization Factor
MV	= Motion Vector
OVQ	= Objective Video Quality Measure
CodTime/DecTime	= Coding/Decoding Time [sec]
CR	= Compression Ratio (compressed/original*100) [%]
Intra	= MPEG-1 Intra-Coding Mode
Inter	= MPEG-1 Inter-Coding Mode
IP	= Picture Pattern IPPP
IB	= Picture Pattern IBBB
BP	= Picture Pattern IBBPBB

7.2.2 Flower Results

	QF	CodTime [s]	DecTime [s]	OVQ	Size [bytes]	CR [%]
Flower	1	420.5	62.8	4.764	11,110,254	48.71
Intra	15	403.8	39.4	4.757	3,402,758	14.92
	31	398.1	34.6	4.726	1,970,939	8.64

	QF	MV	CodTime [s]	DecTime [s]	OVQ	Size [bytes]	CR [%]
Flower	1	1	337.2	51.7	4.764	7,832,709	34.34
Inter	1	8	385.3	51.5	4.764	7,691,681	33.72
IP	1	15	409.4	51.2	4.764	7,669,316	33.62
	15	1	309.3	30.1	4.741	1,977,978	8.67
	15	8	352.9	29.6	4.739	1,864,113	8.17
	15	15	381.7	29.5	4.738	1,845,779	8.09
	31	1	299.3	25.4	4.707	1,065,560	4.67
	31	8	342.4	24.7	4.704	984,128	4.31
	31	15	370.7	24.5	4.704	970,832	4.26

	QF	MV	CodTime [s]	DecTime [s]	OVQ	Size [bytes]	CR [%]
Flower	1	1	476.0	48.2	4.752	6,249,105	27.40
Inter	1	8	656.0	47.1	4.753	5,870,118	25.74
IB	1	15	815.7	46.8	4.753	5,770,479	25.30
	15	1	445.9	27.7	4.710	1,342,061	5.88
	15	8	624.4	26.6	4.703	1,180,581	5.18
	15	15	781.8	26.2	4.703	1,141,191	5.00
	31	1	438.9	24.4	4.675	753,589	3.30
	31	8	616.1	23.3	4.666	660,564	2.90
	31	15	774.3	23.1	4.666	639,079	2.80

	QF	MV	CodTime [s]	DecTime [s]	OVQ	Size [bytes]	CR [%]
Flower	1	1	434.9	51.9	4.758	7,024,420	30.80
Inter	1	8	564.0	50.1	4.758	6,504,593	28.52
BP	1	15	677.8	49.6	4.758	6,340,896	27.80
	15	1	400.3	28.7	4.713	1,327,735	5.82
	15	8	527.4	26.8	4.708	1,091,803	4.79
	15	15	641.2	26.4	4.707	1,022,407	4.48
	31	1	387.4	23.8	4.668	697,771	3.06
	31	8	513.5	22.1	4.663	558,041	2.45
	31	15	627.4	21.5	4.662	517,331	2.27

7.3   Table of H.261 Measurement Results

7.3.1   Market Results

	QF	CodTime [s]	DecTime [s]	OVQ	Size [bytes]	CR [%]
Market	1	344.5	60.9	4.724	16,705,291	73.24
Intra	15	330.5	24.1	4.645	2,194,359	9.62
	31	350.0	21.0	4.593	1,094,959	4.80

	QF	MV	CodTime [s]	DecTime [s]	OVQ	Size [bytes]	CR [%]
Market	1	1	268.3	47.4	4.693	9,711,637	42.58
Inter	1	15	285.9	47.6	4.695	9,630,149	42.22
	1	31	320.6	47.5	4.698	9,623,614	42.19
	15	1	215.8	14.8	4.663	450,004	1.97
	15	15	242.6	15.0	4.661	439,437	1.93
	15	31	294.9	15.0	4.660	437,353	1.92
	31	1	207.2	12.4	4.582	180,238	0.79
	31	15	241.2	12.7	4.578	175,678	0.77
	31	31	310.7	12.7	4.571	174,633	0.77

7.3.2   Flower Results

	QF	CodTime [s]	DecTime [s]	OVQ	Size [bytes]	CR [%]
Flower	1	416.1	57.0	4.758	15,138,798	66.37
Intra	15	409.0	22.6	4.717	1,695,395	7.43
	31	417.6	20.3	4.559	833,536	3.65

	QF	MV	CodTime [s]	DecTime [s]	OVQ	Size [bytes]	CR [%]
Flower	1	1	267.6	47.8	4.759	11,127,513	48.78
Inter	1	15	311.7	49.1	4.758	11,007,861	48.26
	1	31	407.0	50.7	4.761	10,280,615	45.07
	15	1	226.8	18.3	4.715	1,127,435	4.94
	15	15	277.7	19.2	4.718	1,114,897	4.89
	15	31	389.9	20.3	4.702	848,169	3.72
	31	1	222.5	16.2	4.557	532,158	2.33
	31	15	276.8	16.9	4.567	525,295	2.30
	31	31	398.4	17.7	4.546	378,332	1.66

QF	= Quantization Factor
MV	= Motion Vector
OVQ	= Objective Video Quality Measure
CodTime/DecTime	= Coding/Decoding Time [sec]
CR	= Compression Ratio (compressed/original*100) [%]
Intra	= H.261 Intra-Coding Mode
Inter	= H.261 Inter-Coding Mode

Bibliography

[1]   R. Aravind, G.L. Cash, D.L. Duttweiler, H.-M. Hang, B.G. Haskell, A. Puri: Image and video coding standards. AT&T Technical Journal, Jan/Feb 1993

[2]   B. S. Atal, V. Cuperman, A. Gersho (eds.): Speech and Audio Coding for Wireless and Network Applications. Kluwer Academic Publishers, Dordrecht, 1993

[3]   Communications of the ACM, Special Section on Interactive Technology, Vol. 32, No. 7, July 1989

[4]   Communications of the ACM, Special Section on Digital Multimedia Systems, Vol. 34, No. 4, April 1991

[5]   M. F. Barnsley, L. P. Hurd: Fractal Image Compression. AK Peters, Wellesley, Massachusetts, 1993

[6]   G. Blair, D. Hutchison, D. Shepherd: Multimedia systems. Tutorial, Proc. of 3rd IFIP Conference on High-Speed Networking, Berlin, March 18–22, 1991

[7]   W. Effelsberg, B. Lamparter: Extended color cell compression, in. IWACA 1994, Heidelberg, Springer LNCS 868, Springer-Verlag, Berlin, 1994, pp. 181–190

[8]   S. Fischer, R. Lienhart, W. Effelsberg: Automatic recognition of film genres. Proc. ACM Multimedia 95, San Francisco, 1995, pp. 295–304

[9]   Y. Fisher: Fractal Image Compression – Theory and Application. Springer-Verlag, New York, 1995

[10]   F. Fluckiger: Understanding Networked Multimedia – Applications and technology. Prentice-Hall, Upper Saddle River, 1995

[11]   R. M. Gray: Vector Quantization. IEEE ASSP Magazine, Vol. 1, No. 2, April 1984, pp. 4–29

[12]   K. Harney, M. Keith, G. Lavelle, L. D. Ryan, D. J. Stark: The i750 Video Processor – A Total Multimedia Solution. Communications of the ACM, Vol. 34, No. 4, 1991, pp. 64–78

[13]   M. L. Hilton, B. D. Jawerth, A. Sengupta: Compressing still and moving images with wavelets. Multimedia Systems, Vol. 2, No. 5, 1994, pp. 218–227

[14]   P. G. Howard, J. S. Vitter: Practical implementations of arithmetic coding. [Sto92], pp. 85–112

[15]   D. A. Huffman: A method for the construction of minimum redundancy codes. Proc. IRE 40, September 1952, pp. 1098–1101

[16]   N.S. Jayant, Peter Noll: Digital Coding of Waveforms. Prentice-Hall, 1984

[17]   IEEE Journal on Communications, Special Section on Signal Processing and Coding for Recording Channels, Vol. 10, No. 1, January 1992

[18]   IEEE Journal on Communications, Special Section on Speech and Image Coding, Vol. 10, No. 5, June 1992

[19]   ISO IEC JTC 1: Information Technology. All ISO standards are available from your library or your national standards organization (such as ANSI, DIN, AFNOR, etc.)

[20]   ITU-T – International Telecommunication Union – Telecommunication Standardization Sector. All documents are available directly from ITU's bookstore. For more information refer to http://www.itu.ch/itudoc/itu-t

[21]   W. Kou: Digital Image Compression – Algorithms and Standards. Kluwer Academic Publishers, Dordrecht, 1995

[22]   F. Kuo, W. Effelsberg, J. J. Garcia-Luna-Aceves: Multimedia Communications – Protocols and Applications. Prentice-Hall, Upper Saddle River, 1998

[23]   B. Lamparter, W. Effelsberg: X-MOVIE: Transmission and Presentation of Digital Movies under X. Proc. 2nd International Workshop on Network and Operating System Support for Digital Audio and Video, Heidelberg, November 1991, pp.18–19.

[24]   D. Le Gall: MPEG – A Video Compression Standard for Multimedia Applications. Communications of the ACM, Vol. 34, No. 4, April 1991, pp. 46–58

[25]   B. Lamparter, W. Effelsberg, N. Michl: MTP – A Movie Transmission Protocol for Multimedia Applications. Proc. of the 4th IEEE ComSoc International Workshop on Multimedia Communications, Montery, Colifornia, April 1992, pp. 260–270

[26]   E. N. Linzer, E. Feig: New DCT and Scaled DCT Algorithms for Fused Multiply/Add Architectures. Proc. IEEE ICASSP-91, Toronto, Canada, May 1991, pp. 2201–2204

[27]   M. Liou: An Overview of the px64 kbit/s Video Coding Standard. Communications of the ACM, Vol. 34, No. 4, April 1991, pp. 59–63

[28]   R. Lienhart, F. Stuber: Automatic text recognition in digital videos. Image and Video Processing IV 1996, Proc. SPIE 2666–20 (1996)

[29]   R. Lienhart, W. Effelsberg, R. Jain: Towards a Visual Grep: A systematic analysis of various methods to compare video sequences. Storage and Retrieval for Image and Video Databases VI, Ishwar. K. Sethi, Ramesh C. Jain (eds.): Proc. SPIE 3312 (1998), pp. 271–282

[30]   G. Lu: Advances in Digital Image Compression Techniques. Computer Communications, Vol. 16, No. 4, 1993, pp. 202–214

[31]   S.G. Mallat: A Theory for Multiresolution Signal Decomposition. IEEE Trans. Pattern Analysis and Machine Intelligence, Vol. 11, No. 7, 1989, pp. 674–693

[32]   J. L. Mitchell, W. B. Pennebaker: Evolving JPEG Color Data Compression Standard. M. Nier, M. E. Courtot (eds.): Standards for electronic imaging systems, SPIE Vol. CR37, 1991, pp. 68–97

[33]   J. L. Mitchell, W.B. Pennebaker, Ch.E. Fogg, D. LeGall: MPEG Video Compression Standard. Chapman & Hall, New York, 1996

[34]   ISO IEC JTC 1: Information Technology – Coding of Moving Pictures and Associated Audio for Digital Storage Media up to about 1.5Mbit/s. International Standard ISO/IEC IS 11172, 1993

[35] A. N. Netravali, B. G. Haskell: Digital Pictures – Representation and Compression. Plenum Press, New York, 1988

[36] W. B. Pennebaker, J. L. Mitchell, G. Langdon Jr., R.B. Arps: An Overview of the Basic Principles of the Q-Coder Binary Arithmetic Coder. IBM Journal of Research Development, Vol. 32, No. 6, November 1988, pp. 717–726

[37] W. B. Pennebaker, J. L. Mitchell: JPEG Still Image Data Compression. Van Nostrand Reinhold, New York, 1993

[38] S. Pfeiffer, S. Fischer, W. Effelsberg: Automatic Audio Content Analysis. Proc. ACM Multimedia 96, November 1996, pp. 21–30

[39] A. C. Hung: PVRG-JPEG CODEC 1.1, Documentation of the PVRG-JPEG1 Software Codec; Stanford University, California, 1993,
ftp: havefun.stanford.edu:pub/jpeg/JPEGv1.1.tar.Z

[40] A. C. Hung: PVRG-MPEG CODEC 1.1, Documentation of the PVRG-MPEG1 Software Codec; Stanford University, California, 1993,
ftp: havefun.stanford.edu:pub/mpeg/MPEGv1.1.tar.Z

[41] International Telecommunication Union, the International Telegraph and Telephone Consultative Committee; Line Transmission on non-Telephone Signals: Video Codec for Audiovisual Services at px64 kbit/s; CCITT Recommendation H.261, Geneva, 1990

[42] M. Rabbani, P. Jones: Digital Image Compression Techniques. Tutorial Texts in Optical Engineering, Vol. TT7, SPIE Press, 1991

[43] S. J. Solari: Digital Video and Audio Compression. McGraw-Hill, New York, 1997

[44] R. Steinmetz: Human perception of Jitter and Media Synchronization. IEEE JSAC, Vol. 14, No. 1, 1996, pp. 61–72

[45] R. Steinmetz: Multimedia Technology – Fundamentals and Introduction (in German), Springer-Verlag, Berlin, 1993

[46] R. Steinmetz, K. Nahrstedt: Multimedia Computing, Communications and Applications. Prentice-Hall, Upper Saddle River, 1995

[47] J. A. Storer: Data Compression Methods and Theory. Computer Science Press, Rockville, Maryland, 1988

[48] D. Taubman, A. Zakhor: Multirate 3-D Subband Coding of Video. IEEE Trans. Image Processing, Vol. 3, No. 5, 1994, pp. 572–588

[49] Ch. J. van den Branden Lambrecht: A working spatio-temporal model of the human visual system for image restoration and quality assessment applications. Proc. Intl. Conference on Acoustics, Speech and Signal Processing, Atlanta, 1996

[50] G. K. Wallace: The JPEG Still Picture Compression Standard. Communications of the ACM, Vol. 34, No. 4, April 1991, pp. 30–44

[51] A. A. Webster, Coleen T. Jones, Margaret H. Pinson, Stephen D. Voran, Stephen Wolf: An objective video quality assessment system based on human perception. SPIE, Vol. 1913, 1993, pp. 15–26

Index